WINNING C

By the same author

Boatbuilding on a Glass Fibre Hull
Small Boat Building
Buying a Secondhand Boat
Uniweld Data Book
How to be Rich and Successful

'To my wife Sue'

WINNING CONCEPTS

by

Dave Gannaway

published by

Solomon Publications

Donna Dene
Bridge Road
Bursledon
Southampton

First published in 1985 in Great Britain by
Solomon International Publishing Co
Donna Dene, Bridge Road,
Bursledon, Southampton SO3 8AH.

British Library Cataloguing in Publication Data

Gannaway, Dave
Winning concepts.
1. Success
I. Title
158′.1 BF637.S8

ISBN 0-946155-01-1

Typeset by Katerprint Co. Ltd, Oxford
Printed and bound by Itchen Printers Ltd, Southampton

Contents

Preface

The object of this book is to show that success and happiness can be attained by everyone. Indeed, it should be the goal of every human being to be happy, a natural instinct. I do not believe that the Creator put us on this earth, some to succeed and some to fail. We all have the freedom to choose. Indeed acceptance of that very fact presents one of the most fundamental and difficult obstacles many have to overcome before they can begin their journey towards success.

We are unique in the animal kingdom in that we are the only creatures with the ability to control our own destiny. This ability is given to us through the miracle we call our brain. Without fear of contradiction the brain is one of the greatest creations our universe has ever known. Scientists still know very little about the way it works or just where the limits of its abilities lie, if indeed it does have any limits. We do know that we use just the smallest fraction of its potential; and experts in the field estimate that less than one-tenth is used in a normal lifetime.

But everyone has one of those wonderful machines, all to themselves. The brain's ability to conceive ideas and create something from, seemingly, nothing is almost beyond comprehension. So how can we know what wonders this brain of ours can conceive and achieve? That answer is in the very first chapter and it is something all the successful people of the world share – imagination.

I sometimes sit and ponder what wonders the world will be enjoying twenty years from now. And when it is considered what developments have taken place over the past twenty years it becomes more than one person can comprehend. The prospect is so exciting that the opportunities opening up for those with imagination are literally out of this world.

So with all these exciting prospects, what can we do to achieve success, to use more of the amazing gifts we already have, to take advantage of some of the treasures the world has to offer? The answers are well within your reach if you have the mind to grasp them.

Teaching the brain to perform those tasks required to achieve our goals and dreams is the very purpose of this book. By understanding one fact – that the brain can do whatever it decides to do – you are over the biggest single hurdle between you and success. Ensure your brain understands that you are a success and your brain will, without question, provide you with that success.

The key, the miracle, is within you. Follow the advice that is give herein and the author's basic explanation will reveal the simple mysteries to you. Master them and success will be yours.

Author's Note

Onc of the reasons why so many folk live out their days without experiencing the real thrill of success is simply because they have not stopped to wonder what success is for them. So many have lived their lives struggling from day to day, giving no thought or concern to their future other than to simply get by. Life itself is a drudge, a rut that they have long since got into, leaving them numb to all but the basic instincts.

It is a sad fact that many people in that situation are just not receptive to help. "Why should anyone want to help me?" they say. Why, indeed? But it is that built-in negative outlook that provides the pattern of their future and, sadly, without question they are on the downward path.

Have you ever felt that the pattern of your life is like driving UP the DOWN lane of the motorway? Where it seems everything and everyone is going against you? Understand, you can get out of that situation. You can quickly turn around – change direction – get in tune with the success pattern.

Failure patterns can and must be reversed. You too can reach and achieve happiness if you have the mind to. If we sat together now, you and I, I would be able to steer you in the right direction. There is no doubt in my mind about that, provided that success is what YOU want. Let me do it now through the medium of words.

The only link between us, you and I, are the printed words on these pages and whilst we may be denied personal contact I hope my sincerity will reach you through these pages.

You CAN stop negative traits and failures NOW. Look in the mirror and see yourself as successful and remember always that 'You can if you think you can.'

Chapter 1

Goals and Dreams

Why start the first chapter of a new book with goals and dreams? Well the reason is very simple, because without them life has no purpose, or reason. Without our goals and dreams we would all be alike, we would all be wallowing in the same muddy rut, existing from day to day without reason or purpose.

Some whose lives have not been as rich as they would have liked, give me a look of disbelief when I say that anything is possible if you really want it badly enough.

"So you think we WANT to fail?" answered a Mr Typical.

"No, I'm sure you don't want to fail, but because you don't understand the importance of planning your future and setting your goals you are passing up the opportunities."

"What's the point of dreaming? It only upsets everyone," he said.

"Everything worthwhile starts with a dream or desire. That is the very moment of creation, the moment you realize that YOU could achieve those things – if you really wanted to."

"Ahhh, all those fancy words, but I'm still broke."

"Yes, but once you can see that, you need not be

broke. Once you understand and believe that, you can achieve so much more. You can if you think you can."

"There you go again, but I'm still broke."

"Just believe you can and you will be over the biggest hurdle. Say and believe you CAN and you will overcome being broke," I said.

"Then what?"

"Then decide what your goals are, what you want."

"I want to be stinkin' rich!"

"That's not enough. That is just wishful thinking, like a child wishing to be set loose in a sweet shop. Now tell me, what kind of things would you really like to own and achieve?"

"Car, I s'pose."

"What type of car?"

"I don't care, anything with wheels."

"That's not good enough. You need to know exactly what you want right down to the last detail."

How often have you heard this type of conversation? It's a standard that I hear so often.

Without goals and dreams your life could consist of simply getting through each day and on to the next, with nothing to look forward to or to strive for. Resigned to a future of nothing more than the nothing you have right now. A life your children could inherit which could mean that by following in your footsteps their lives could be full to the brim with nothing.

I'm Excited

Millions of people are already like that. They are already dead in a manner of speaking. All they are waiting for is death itself. You must know people like that; I know I do and it makes me sad, because so much is possible if only they could find a dream. But I'm excited because although

I can't help all of those people – because they do not want to be helped – I can help YOU. You, the person reading this book. I want you to come with me through the pages of this book and let me explain some of the processes that will help you to set dreams and make them come true. Because you can, you know. Let me show you.

Ask most people, "Do you have a dream?" and you are likely to get the answer, "Only when I eat pickled onions before going to bed!" or "Yes, but I can never remember them when I wake up!" Well, of course, that is not the type of dreams I am referring to. I am going to talk about dreams of the future. Goals and dreams, the reason for striving and stretching. Your plans for the future.

The past is dead and gone, there is nothing we can do about that, so to worry and fret about 'what should or could have been' or 'why your life has not been a success up to now', is a frustrating waste of time. It really doesn't matter, it has gone and all the worrying in the world will not make the slightest difference.

Dare to Say 'I Can'

I meet many people who are fascinated by my writing activities and it is amazing how many of those people say, "I've often wanted to write", or "I've often wondered if I had what it takes to be a writer?"

"Do you know what it takes to find out?" I always answer.

"What?" Their ears prick up, waiting for some magical explanation.

"A pen and paper. All you need to do is write." What could be easier?

So many people are frustrated writers, painters, singers, musicians etc. and they waste their lives wondering, but never knowing, if they could have done it, if they could have been a success. For most I think the reason is a fear of failing or even a fear of success. But if only they would dare to say "I CAN" many would discover that all of life is open to them. How will you ever know unless you try?

When you understand that the majority of people you rub shoulders with in your everyday life are thoroughly negative and resigned to doing nothing with their lives you will see the danger. Because if you mix with that type of person, very soon you will become like that yourself. You are receiving such a bombardment of negatives that it is inevitable that you will become negative.

What is important now is to make a new and positive start. Take off the failure hat of the past and pitch it into the dustbin and slam the lid down fast. Because from this time on you are going to change. From the time you arrive at the end of this chapter you will be committed to change lanes. You are going to move over into the fast lane because by then you will have a destination, a goal, a dream and you need to be in the fast lane because you are in a hurry to get there. Too much time has been lost and wasted already. Fill up your fuel tank, take a flask and lunch-box because you'll not be having much time to stop or to cruise from now on.

You're Excited

Already you are becoming excited at the prospects and possibilities that lie ahead. Keep excited and enthusiastic and the journey will be fast and fascinating. Feel the excitement tingling through your body, keep it like that, and you will soon notice that people will begin to turn their heads when you pass. You will be noticed because that type of excitement and enthusiasm radiates from your very soul. It's a happiness that is contagious.

Invisible though it may be, you will be in no doubt that it is there with you.

People like to be around winners and excited people, it's fun for everyone, because everyone loves to be happy. You will develop an aura of confidence that grows stronger and stronger as you become more and more successful. Have you ever been in a room when someone comes in filling the whole room with his presence? See yourself like that, because that is how it will be. But more about that later.

Everyone should have dreams and goals. That is what life is all about. Striving, stretching and achieving. Mothers have dreams for their children, the businessman should have dreams for the expansion and success of his company. Road diggers, doctors, boatbuilders or barristers, everyone needs a dream. And without a dream they will stay on the bottom line vegetating, and if they are not already there, they soon will be. It's impossible to stand still – you must either go on or go back.

Never Give Up

But when you are excited the choice is already made, you will never consider going back. It will never even enter your head. In fact, you will often learn to 'burn your bridges' so that you can't turn back. You must keep going no matter what. Set your goals and commit yourself to do whatever is required to achieve them. But never never stop until you succeed. Remember the great Sir Winston Churchill's famous speech before our finest hour? "NEVER – NEVER – NEVER – GIVE UP." You can get no wiser advice than that. There is no magical formula, no secret spell or chanting phrase that can make your dreams come into fulfilment. You need to work for them. You have to earn them to have the right to them and when you do those dreams and goals become achievements that mean so much more. It's a process that makes you a better person into the bargain.

It just would not mean the same thing if I were to be able to make all your dreams appear in a sprinkling of stardust, as they do in Disney movies, but I can break the process down into a series of simple steps, each step being designed to lead you on to the next and advancing you another step towards your goals and dreams. This is the quickest route to take and it is important to your progress as a person. You see, success is the 'person'. Material possessions, such as cars, houses, aircraft, etc., are just the perks. They are just some of the benefits that go with success, but money and possessions are a measure of success, not success itself.

Status v. Wealth

Many become confused with the difference between status and wealth. Let me try to define the difference. Compare, for instance, a bank manager and a wealthy man and you may begin to see this difference. The bank manager is the one with the pin-stripe suit, a smart office and status. He has money passing through his hands all the time. He is the person people woo when they are looking for a loan, etc. He has the power to grant or deny your request.

The money the bank manager handles is the tool of his trade. It's not his money. He has been entrusted to use it to make a profit, but it is not his money. Many such people may be of modest means.

Some years ago I found myself as director of a large company, with a smart car, big office, secretary, board meetings, trips abroad, expense accounts, etc. Most people assumed I owned the company, I was the envy of my friends. They thought I had arrived, that I'd hit the 'jack pot'. Wrong. The salary was nothing to write home about, the smart car was a company car which would never be mine – if I upset them they could take it away at a stroke. The expense account was simply a little extra money with which to handle company business. Another expression of status.

For me it was all a façade and a very insecure situation. It was also a period when I made very little personal growth. Everyone was amazed and called me crazy when I decided to move on. But move on I did, and how glad I am now. It was J. Paul Getty, one of the world's wealthiest men, who said; "The only way to be wealthy is to work for yourself." How true that is. When you think about it, no matter who your boss is, he will never allow a situation where you earn more than he does, human nature being what it is.

Stretch

You will learn how to stretch and lift your horizons beyond the four walls that have been your castle and keep up until now. You will liberate the most incredible machine yet known to man to work exclusively for you – your brain.

As you learn to stretch you will find yourself including in your dreams and goals those things only considered possible by other people before. You will liberate your brain and give it free rein to complete the tasks you set for it, because your brain is literally the nerve centre of everything. It is the bridge, the cockpit, the satellite communications system and power plant all rolled into one. "Ask and it shall be given unto you" – and it is the brain that will make it all possible.

"Oh," you may say, "but I never was one of those

brainy types." Don't worry, if you lack education it makes no difference. You will simply choose a route that does not require education. It is quite true, education does help people to get jobs but it is far from a guarantee for success. I know many well-educated people who are always broke and worrying how they are going to meet next month's bills. They often have important jobs that pay very little money and restrict their freedom, and these are two of the most precious commodities of all.

One of your goals may be to get a special job or become more advanced in the job you have. If that is the case, fine, nothing wrong with that. So long as it is what you really want. But if your goals and dreams include wealth and expensive acquisitions then you don't need a boss. You just need YOU and a healthy business of your own to take you where you need to go.

People who are failures are in that position simply because they 'gave up' or never even tried. Their goals were either non-existent or they were not big or important enough. People with real goals never give up, Oh, they may get knocked down once or twice along the road, but you can be sure that they will get up and finish the job. That is the true quality of a winner.

How Much can Money Buy?

As you become more successful you will hear it said, "Oh, you can't buy everything!" or "Money isn't everything." Both statements are true to some degree but the person who speaks those words is simply making an excuse for not having become successful himself. He is saying "I can't make it, so it doesn't matter." True there are some things that money can't buy. Health, for instance, the joy of children, and love are typical examples. But the presence or lack of money has little to do with those anyway.

The hard fact is that with money you can do so much more than you can without it. I have heard it said that money cannot buy happiness, but it can, you know. Consider the happiness you could spread if you had money to spare. You will find, I am sure, that people who make statements like, "Money can't buy everything," are those who don't have any. A rich man has the privilege to give help and assistance to whomever or whatever he wishes. A poor man is denied that privilege, he needs all he has to survive, himself.

Within our society, like it or not, success is generally calibrated in terms of money. Whether this is right or wrong is a matter of opinion. My only concern is that, to be successful in this real world today requires hard cash. Money is the universal passport, the credentials to your material goals. For me money itself it not my ultimate objective; achieving my most cherished goal, true and real freedom, is the main ingredient, and for most it is the key to liberty and sovereignty over your own life.

Goals

See your life on a giant screen in your brain. Select and decide what you want in your life and place it on that screen. This is very important because there are only two choices:

A. Those who control. Be master of your own life. (FREEDOM)

B. Those who are controlled. Let someone else be master of your life. (HAVE A JOB)

Type A's are the winners who are in control. The leaders who make the rules for the B's to follow.

Type B's are those who have a boss or employer to answer to and have their whole life controlled, run by circumstances beyond their control. This type of person is the worker bee.

What Type Are You?

The first, group A, has control. They know exactly where they are going and what they are going to do. Their minds are open to opportunities and new ideas. They will 'Have a go', try new things with enthusiasm and an open mind. Then, once they are sure the idea will work, they will make the commitment and go. Then, and this shows the true quality of the person, they will stick to the plan until its successful conclusion. They are the winners.

Type B represents the majority who spend their lives waiting for the right opportunity to come along, or waiting until the 'time is right'. They often say, "If only I could have a business of my own," "If only I had a little more money," "If only I could afford a new car," if only, if only, if only. When the opportunity presents itself they say, "That looks great, I'll have a go at that, once my holidays are over or first thing after Christmas." They always have an excuse, a very good reason why they should NOT do it.

One Choice

So what types of goals and dreams should you set for yourself? Naturally everyone will choose different things. Let's have a look at some of them. Maybe your goals and dreams will depend upon your physical condition. It could be to run a marathon or a hundred yards dash in record time. Or could it be to skate, swim, walk, box, ski, surf, climb, sail, or ride?

What about the group that deals with business and financial dreams and goals. Could your dream be to own a business of your own that has a turnover of a million pounds? Or could it be to have a personal fortune of a million? It could be to follow on where Onassis left off or to pump more oil than the late J. Paul Getty. The list is endless.

Sit quietly and think about it. Have a notepad to hand. Write down any ideas that come to mind. This is the start of the goal and dream-setting process. From notes such as these your true goals will emerge, but the more ideas you have written down the easier it will be.

See yourself with these goals. Visualize yourself in situations that involve the thing you like doing and would like to own. Shake off any restrictions you may normally have. If you want to own a jet, then write it down and picture yourself scorching about the skies as free as an eagle. Goals are a challenge, so set them high, give yourself something to stretch for. And believe with all your heart that you will be the owner of these things.

Dream in Reality

Just learn to dream in reality. Dream of obtainable goals. By this I do not mean that you should place restrictions on yourself. No, I mean simply dream for things that can be achieved. It would be as silly to dream of becoming King of Siam or even the Queen of England as it would be to be the owner of Westminster Cathedral or Buckingham Palace. We are not dealing in fantasies, we are dealing with a world full of real things and real people that is here waiting today. So dream achievable dreams.

Do what it Takes

Get excited and enthusiastic about it and become resigned to going out and doing 'whatever it takes' to achieve it. Once you accept that simple premise that you are prepared to go out and do whatever it takes, then you have the main ingredient for success. Given these conditions you will find that you will bring out the best in yourself and begin to operate on a higher level than ever before.

Look out for the petty aggravations that you will encounter along the way. Because even in the most well thought out situation there are always snags and you can be sure that someone will put out their foot and try to trip you up. If you are aware that this can happen you can be ready for it when it happens and step over the obstruction and avoid stumbling.

Setting out on the road to your goals is exciting and the bigger the goals the more exciting the process, as a lone voyager feels when he sets out to cross the ocean unaware of what problems and setbacks may befall him. You will be the same, but once you have set out and the goals are set and commitments made, nothing will stop you. NOTHING. Problems that befall the lone sailor in mid-ocean he will overcome in whatever way he can. He is in the situation and the only way out is to fight on. His bridges are burned, so he can't go back. No, the only way is to fight and move on. Just do what it takes to keep going.

Winners Never Give Up

One thing you can be sure of is that a winner will never turn back or give in. He may get knocked down a dozen times but each time he will get up. He'll never, never give up. Sure, there will be times when you will feel down and fed-up and tempted to turn back, but you know full well that you will not because that would mean defeat and defeat in any form is unthinkable.

It is worth noting that if the lone sailor's goal was not to sail the ocean but a lake or smaller goal, he would probably have foreseen those problems awaiting him and the chances are that he would never have even set out at all. For this very reason it is wise to set yourself big goals and big dreams. There is no difference in sailing a little ocean or a big ocean, it just takes a little longer. The same applies to a building: there is little difference in building a single-storied bungalow or a 10 storey block of flats, except that the bricklayers have to keep going longer.

Goal Setting – How to Set Your Goals

I've heard it said that there is more to setting goals than to achieving them. And that is simply because people need to know 'how' – just as it is easy to ride a bicycle once you know how. The secret is to be in no doubt whatsoever that you *can* do it. Have confidence and believe *totally* that you can and will do what is required.

Making a goal or dream is setting a challenge for yourself. A challenge that you cannot refuse, a commitment so strong that the only way out is by achievement.

Goals are like Eggs

Your goals are like eggs, they come in large, medium, and small sizes and are nothing until they are 'cracked'. The most positive way to set a big goal is to break it down into small bites or small goals. How do you climb a mountain? One step at a time. The same skill is required for walking 50 yards as it is for walking a mile – you just keep walking longer. And it is the same for anything. How should you live your life? One day at a time. How do you reach your big goals? One small goal at a time.

Imagine, for a moment, that your goal is to own or build a beautiful yacht. That goal on its own is not good enough. It is too broad, too general. There must be more detail. I remember asking a young man what he would do if I gave him £2,000! His answer was that he would jet himself off for a holiday in the sun. But you see, his answer is too broad, there is not enough detail. What would happen if he arrived at London International Airport, made his way to the booking office and said, "One ticket to the sun, please." I'm sure the lady behind the desk would fall on the floor laughing. He needs more detail. He should be able to say, "One ticket to Miami on the 5th August; please arrange a booking at the Fort Lauderdale Hilton for 7 days with a room overlooking the sea and I'd like a Ford Mustang hire car waiting for me at the airport when I arrive." Now he knows what he wants. He has the details. The more details the better.

Write everything down, look at the relative catalogues and brochures to help with details, construct enough details to be able to actually DO it, because that is exactly what you are going to do. This is the very foundation of your success, it is the reason for what you are doing.

Other goals may be smaller but treat them in the same way. See them clearly and write down every detail as it occurs to you. Whilst defining your goals and dreams you should open your mind to all possibilities. Anything is possible.

Fly High

I took my eldest son for a joyride in an aeroplane, for a treat. He enjoyed the experience so much and it gave him such a buzz that he just had to learn how to fly himself. He thought of nothing else but flying. It took over his whole life. Every penny he owned and earned went towards another flying lesson. Now, twelve months later, he has just passed out as a qualified pilot. In fact, he took me flying just the other day and I must say that I felt his buzz too.

He had a dream. He saw himself up there at the controls of an aeroplane. He had no doubt at all what he was going to do. The only question was how long it was going to take him to do it, and how to pay for it. Though that success is behind him, he is now formulating yet higher goals. Now he wants to own the aircraft!

You can set anything as your goal. Maybe you don't hanker to jet about the skies or to sail the oceans. Your dream could be to own a beautiful home and garden, where you can simply 'potter' around and just take life easy. Or your goal could be just to have the time to enjoy what you already have, to spend time with your wife and family or just stay at home and enjoy doing nothing!

Have fun thinking and writing your list. Get excited and enthusiastic. Don't let anything restrict your thinking. Just let your imagination run free. Try to set those goals 30% higher than you require. Like a glass of lemonade, make allowance for the froth on top. So that if you want a full glass of lemonade you add 30% more to top up the glass when the froth disappears.

Small Goals

Don't forget small goals because they help to keep interest and enthusiasm alive on the way to the big goals. Big goals are often a collection of small goals. Just as a house is built with a collection of bricks. It is also a proven fact that success breeds success, so by achieving your smaller goals you are also helping yourself along to your big goals.

Small goals come thick and fast once you really start. But don't stop the flow. It doesn't matter how long your list is, what is more important is to get everything down on paper; it is very important to write everything down.

Let's look at some small goals. A friend of mine bought himself a sit-on mower to keep his lawn in trim, then he discovered that when he was out cutting the grass he could not hear his telephone ringing. So his next little goal was a cordless phone that could travel with him on the mower. And there are other goals. For instance, what about more holidays abroad, a gardener, swimming pool, horse, expensive car, a villa in the sun or even a special night out with the family? Keep writing your list until you run dry.

Then you have an important job to do. The next stage is to take the list and rewrite it, putting everything in its correct order. Starting with the most important items and ending with the least.

This task is not so easy as you might imagine. It is something that could take a little time to do because you will swop and change things about, not just once but repeatedly. This is all part of the process. Do it no matter how long it takes. Keep at it until you have one long list with the most important items at the top descending in order of priority.

Find the Problem

The next stage in our goal setting programme is to take them one at a time, again starting with the most important goal, and list the reason why you have not already achieved them. What is stopping you? What is holding you back? Ask questions. Make yourself answer. This is so important because at last you are about to uncover the real problem, the real reason why success has eluded you so far.

Question your own answers, interrogate yourself. Search deeply for those all-important clues and answers. Let's take a simple example:

Goal A NEW SILVER JAGUAR XJ6

A. Why have I not achieved this goal?
   1. LACK OF MONEY
   2. OPPORTUNITY
   3. NEVER DARED

B. What solutions could there be to A?
   1. EARN MORE MONEY
   2. IMPROVE JOB OR PROSPECT
   3. DARE TO SUCCEED

C. What solution could there be to B?
   (Free the mind of anything that may restrict the imagination)
   1. OWN A BUSINESS OF YOUR OWN
   2. OWN A BUSINESS OF YOUR OWN
   3. OWN A BUSINESS OF YOUR OWN

So, as you can see, posing and answering your own questions can reveal, or give a good idea of, what the problem is. If you keep searching, the solution will show itself. In this case, section B reveals and suggests to me that the search must begin for something better by way of income. Whatever form it takes you need more money. That, in turn, means 1. Looking for a better paying job, or 2. Searching for a second income, hopefully one that has sufficient prospects and potential to allow it, in the future, to take over your main job, thus lifting your life-style without risking the present income. 3. Be a little more ambitious, raise the sights, square your shoulders and have more confidence. Dare to speak your worth, then demand it.

The real answer, in my opinion, is revealed in section C. Starting a business of your own. Taking action in that direction could provide the answer, not only to this single goal, but to many of the others that may follow.

Very often it will be found that by simply writing the problem down as set out above the answer becomes glaringly obvious. Or what also often happens is that all the problems can be solved by a single solution. But whatever comes out of it you will be able to see clearly exactly what the solution is. Very often you will be amazed how simple and obvious it is, and you will kick yourself for not having spotted it earlier. But that is the advantage of writing everything down, it allows you to look at familiar problems from a different viewpoint.

Once you have identified the problem you are well on your way up the ladder of success. Because once you can identify and accept that there is a problem, something holding you back, you can positively set about doing something about it. You may not like this section of the plan because it is most revealing, but it can't be ignored, and it's great for character building. Face up to it squarely. Only you need see the results, but it is vital that you have this information. And it is upon this information that you will begin to work right now by eliminating the nasties.

Come to terms with the fact that you are not perfect; none of us are, we would all be so boring if we were, but if there are some things about your make-up, physical or psychological, that are holding back your real progress then you must be strong enough to find out what they are and stamp them out. Then you can go back to the job in question with both hands free and not, as before, with one hand tied behind your back.

Start working on this now, today, you'll be a better person as a result. We will be looking more closely at some of the reasons and problems in later chapters.

Just a Word About the Joneses

Winners have no need to keep up with the Joneses. They are leaders in their own right. They see themselves as top of the pile, as pace-setters. So try not to let petty negatives sneak in and spoil your victory. Stretch and rise above that. You will be a bigger person if you can rise above that.

Success can bring out unpleasant traits in your character, if you allow it to. So, beware. I've often seen great success clouded by arrogance towards the less fortunate, towards those still struggling up the ladder. It's common enough to see people build a great castle with their success. A castle complete with keep, battlements and moat, to keep all-comers out. The owners can often be seen peeping over the top or even pouring boiling oil over anyone whose ladder of success even approaches their doorway. And although quite common, it is still very sad.

Let me give an example of what I mean. Imagine yourself very successful, imagine you did own a castle of your own complete with everything that goes with it plus a beautiful Rolls-Royce to top it off. Would success for you be to drive your beautiful car inside the castle grounds, lift the drawbridge and shut off the world outside? Few would know about your success and those who did would soon grow to despise you.

Would it not be more fun and so much more satisfying to invite your friends to ride in your beautiful Rolls-Royce with you and to visit your lovely castle? The result would be that you earned their love and respect. Success is as much about giving as receiving.

In the next chapter I will be dealing with the most important personal quality and the true secret of success, that one single thing without which real success is impossible. Next to knowing what success is for you, a positive 'self-image' is the vital link, often the missing link, in the process that leads to your success.

Points from this chapter:

- Get excited
- Never give up
- Status *v.* wealth
- Stretch
- Do whatever it takes
- How to set your goals

Chapter 2

Self-Image

If I could write only one chapter on the subject of motivation and self help it would be on the topic of 'self-image', because most often this is the area where the barrier to success is erected. Many struggle on through their lives overcoming one problem after another; they read all the right books and follow the success road, yet things still seem to fall short of the target. Maybe you can identify with that. It is quite likely that you are doing everything that is required; you have the winning concept, but your self-image is letting you down, It is quite natural to look outside ourselves for the shortcomings but more often than not the answer is to be found within ourselves.

If your life is not yet successful or not producing the income or rewards you know you are worth, you must discover what is missing, what you are doing wrong or maybe not doing at all. Then you must change things. First discover what the problem is, then put it right. If somewhere in your make-up there is something – a quality or trait – that is standing in the way of your success – well, it must be found and changed.

Imagine, if you will, the great allied armies gathered together ready for the D-Day landings. The very best of everything is gathered together; ships, aircraft, tanks, guns and equipment, plus the finest Generals, Captains and Other Ranks available. The best the free world could muster. At the head of the gathered armies Sir Winston Churchill stands, the figurehead, the very symbol of everything the gathering armies are offering their lives to protect. That one man headed the motivation force of that, now historic, operation. Just one man. Imagine the self-image he needed.

True he had the best of everything, he had Kings and Princes, Presidents and Emperors behind him. But just one man was responsible for co-ordinating the whole thing. See yourself like that. See your self-image as Churchill, the vital link. But instead of invading the coast of France your target is set on success. You are the link, the lifeline that makes everything work, brings everything together, makes the things you want out of life happen. It's that important.

You may be the owner of the richest land on earth and you can own the finest seeds that money can buy, but if you don't bring those two essentials together nothing will happen. The rich land will yield only weeds and the seeds will remain in the sacks until they rot. You are the link that is required to bring them together, and your self-image is that vital link between you and the success you are striving for.

Read and digest this chapter, dear reader, read and re-read it until you conceive the fact that without the proper self-image there will be no success. Strong words? Certainly, but I cannot impress upon you strongly enough the importance of a proper self-image.

The Brain

Within that wonderful mechanism we call the brain are lurking two people, two characters – they are both you.

They are the two sides of your character, your self-image – Mr. Smart and Mr. Dumb, Mr. Stop and Mr. Go, Mr. Positive and Mr. Negative, call them what you will. But since the brain is the very nerve centre of your whole life, these two images are key figures in your progress. They are the motivating force and regulator of your very exsistence, the thing that sets the brain into motion, gets it into the right gear, fires-up the motor, decides 'Yes, I will do that' or, 'No, I won't.'

That important thing is your self-image, the view and opinion you have of yourself. Understand that it is quite impossible to become better than you think you are. Before you can improve yourself, before anything at all will happen, you must first think and see yourself as a success

Both sides of your self-image are present all the time. The dominant side becomes the master. That is the image we have of ourselves, right now. It is how we are, right now. Hence the expression, 'You can if you think you can', and 'What the mind can conceive and believe, it can achieve'.

In a staggering 95% of the population the dominating side of their self-image is thoroughly negative, Mr. Dumb and Mr. Stop. Most often this image is not of their own choice but is the victim of environment and the process of growing up.

Imagine a little boy in the garden with his father. His father is digging and the boy wants to do the same, he wants to get dirty and dig a hole.

"Get out of my way, kid, you'll never be able to do this, this is man's work." His father yells at him for getting under his feet. Or maybe it was a little girl who tries to help Mummy to make a cake. "Oh, come out from under my feet, you don't understand how to make a cake, you're just a little girl."

Simple little things like that, quite unimportant in

themselves but they bend the child's ego a little, causing a little hurt and the episode is stored away within the brain. That type of thing happens to everyone; it is almost unavoidable. Most often just a careless use of words. No more.

When something like that happens again, that too is stored away in the brain and added to the same file. Over the years that file of rejections and rebukes begins to grow and grow. As it does there comes a time when you begin to realize that your memory file is getting very fat with its store of rejections, rebukes and hurtful words that have been fired at you. Then you begin to question yourself. "Am I a little inferior to the others?" "Why do I always do things wrong?" And it is from this point that you have an in-built inferiority complex. It begins to grow, and feed upon all this stored negative material, gathering more and more (often imagined) material as it goes.

Subconciously the brain begins to say, "All of those people who 'bawled' me out can't be wrong, I must be a failure." The process continues and the longer it does the more you become convinced that you aren't fitted to do this or that, and the pattern of your inferiority and negative life continues to form and grow.

Through school, at the youth club, in your first job, anything that is said to you by way of complaint or criticism becomes accepted and added to the original list. All the while you are growing more and more convinced of your inferiority to everyone else.

At school sports even coming an honest second in the hundred-yard dash is seen, by the self-image, as yet another failure, as never being quite 'good enough'. This eventually has such an effect that you even stop considering that you *can* win, *can* be a leader, *can* be a tremendous success. So your chances of doing so are dashed even before you try. Sadly some people are so conditioned to the negative that they don't even consider trying to succeed any longer, so success for them is out of the question.

Stop the Rot

So what can you do about it? First you must understand and convince that brain of yours that YOU can be whatever you want to be, and that you can have those things you have dreamed of. You CAN achieve those things if you really want to. But you must understand this very important point about the inferiority complex that has been blocking the way until now.

Understand that the inferiority complex, that negative file your brain has stored up over the years, was made by mistake. Your Dad didn't say that you were no good, that you would never be able to dig holes; he was tired and weary. He wanted to get the job finished so that he could have his tea. Did the thought occur to you that he didn't want you to hurt yourself or fall in the hole? And your mother didn't mean that you would never be able to make a cake. You were getting under her feet, she was tired and hot, she was rushing to get the cakes in the oven before she had to start on Dad's tea. Maybe she was even afraid that you would burn yourself. One thing is for sure, they loved you too much to knowingly say anything to hurt you.

What you saw was born of your childish viewpoint. At the time I am sure things did look like that. But looking back now, try to see it in its true perspective. This type of thing happens all the time, most often to young people, so you really are no different to anyone else. Those negative thoughts really were put there by mistake. Believe me, it's true.

You must understand that important point, come to terms with it, and pitch-out all those inferiority and negative images before you can begin to make real progress with a true positive self-image.

Love Yourself

You must learn how to love yourself! Yes, fall in love with yourself! The Bible tells us to love thy neighbour as thy self. So if you don't love yourself, how can you do that? If you don't love yourself it is going to be very difficult to love other people and if you don't do that then you are into a negative situation again.

You must believe and understand that YOU are the most important person you will ever know. The person you actually know is your self-image, that is how YOU see yourself, not how you are seen by others. Read that last sentence again and understand it.

For example, you may have failed at some small thing or other – maybe you failed to get a job you went after, or failed to catch a fish when you went fishing. As a result your whole ego suffers. Just because one little thing goes wrong, you dash your whole self-image. Again, your brain continues to collect all those negatives into one great big heap and the bigger the heap becomes the more resolute you are about your failure image.

Your failure image, inferiority complex, is the result of believing, convincing your brain, that you are a failure. Remember, 'you are what you think you are'. If you believe that everything you do will fail, then it surely will. If you believe that you are destined to a life of failure, then failure is exactly what you will get. 'What the mind can conceive and believe it can surely achieve.' I make no apologies for repeating that quote. So if you are concerned with nothing but failure, that is what you will achieve, because that is what you want.

Think failure and you will be a failure. Think success and you will become a success. Be in no doubt about the wisdom of those words.

Choose to Improve

How can you improve your self-image? Imagine this – you are the subject of the 'This is Your Life' programme. For those readers who are unfamiliar with TV, it is a programme where an interesting, often famous personality is unsuspectingly confronted by a presenter and a collection of family and friends gathered to pay homage to the surprised subject.

Imagine you are the subject and you sit in front of everyone who is important to you and you listen to them telling the world all about you. How you are the kindest friend a person could ever have – the most loyal and cherished companion – you are one of the smartest people ever to do (whatever it is you do!) – how much fun it is to be in your company – describing you as the stimulating and inspiring character you really are.

You know the speakers are sincere, because they are people you respect and love; you know the comments come from the heart. What do you think would happen? Whatever you did you would suddenly be better at it. Your self-image and confidence would rise to new heights. You would, at least, accept your own success and all of a sudden you would BELIEVE in yourself, and you would have a proper self-image.

But think about that for a moment. By the time everyone had completed their appraisal and edification of you, you would feel ten feet tall, so confident you could burst! Yet strangely you are exactly the same person. Nothing has changed since the programme. The only difference is that now you have a proper self-image, you now believe and feel good about yourself, probably for the first time in your life.

Build on those successes, and every other success you have ever had in your life, however small. They are all successes – develop on from them, keep the momentum going. Use them as the vital positive foundation stones for your success.

Hold a vision of that programme in your brain, remind yourself of some of the positive things you have done, forget negatives (you never heard any of those on the programme!), build yourself up. Feel the confidence and self-image increasing. Then, once you have felt the success you will be able to recall the feeling of exhilaration. Then you will begin to control your self-image and your climb up the success ladder will have progressed a little further.

Four Steps to Change

So we have established that almost everyone begins their life with an inferiority complex. That's fine, but let's be positive: what can you do about it? Take heart, because self-image can be changed. It is something you have complete control over. You are the boss, it is your self-image, you gave yourself the wrong one, so now you need to trade it in for a proper one. You can change yourself to how you really wnat to be. So if you look in the mirror and are not happy with what you see, then CHANGE THE IMAGE. You are the master.

So how do we set about it? If you were a motor car you would be traded in for a better model. But since you are a beautiful human being with everything in perfect shape and in perfect working order, all that is really required is a full service and change of oil to enable you to change things about a little and for the first time restructure your self-image to how you see yourself, how you want to be. Refuse to accept that how you are now is how you must remain. It's time to change.

It is an obvious observation that if you don't change something, then it will remain the same, negative and a failure. So how can a change be brought about ? Try this:

Here are the steps to take:

1. Understand that your self-image can be changed. The negative one you have was created out of a misunderstanding and error and it can be changed easily.
2. Construct the plan of how you are going to be, form a detailed mental picture of yourself. Add as much detail as possible. Mentally 'see' yourself as you would like to be. Build the image up piece by piece, work at it, plan it carefully, until your own self-image fulfils your plan. This picture of how you see yourself will change the pattern of your whole life, so treat it seriously and think it out carefully.
3. Write everything down.
4. Once you have your new self-image, be that person every day, begin to 'act-out' the new you. Get to know and make friends with him. Learn to love him and get to enjoy being him because that person will become you. Start from now. Discover that the new you is the real you. That is how you are now, and how you will always be from this moment on. Think of it as your real self surfacing for the first time in your life. At last, after a whole lifetime the real you has emerged, transformed into what God meant you to be, a confident successful person, like a beautiful butterfly emerging from its ugly caterpillar stage.

See that successful person, yourself, clearly in your

mind's eye. See it in a multi-dimensional, coloured, moving picture that is complete in every detail. See yourself in all of the dimensions, feel what it is like to be the new you, feel the buzz of confidence, experience the air of success you radiate. Experience everything about the new you because that is how you are from this moment.

Make a New Start

Now start your life with the new you and do only the things that the new you would do. Let go of old habits and let new ones form naturally. You are a success now. From this moment on your life must change if success is to be yours. Without change things will continue as they were, yielding nothing but negatives and failure. If your life has not yielded the success you desire, you have no option but to change. The path to success runs another route: you must find that route and change NOW.

Never, never forget that from this moment on you are a positive, successful person, and the sooner you can convince your brain of that the sooner positive and successful things will begin to happen for you. Remember these important words, 'You are what you think you are.' Never have truer words been written. Set this book down for a moment and take the time to write them down for yourself. Engrave them upon your mind and never forget that, 'You are what you think you are.'

The Real You

See yourself with that new self-image, the real you that has been trying to get out all this time, discover and convince yourself and your brain that this is at last the real you. Tell your brain that you have now arrived and will now be taking up residence in your right and proper place, as a success.

Now that you have found that exciting new self-image take care to protect it. Stop putting yourself down. You have a new confidence now, learn to love yourself. Oh, I don't mean become conceited, but take a good look in the mirror, move in close, look yourself in the eyes and say, "You are not such a bad guy. I could get to love you." When you come to think about it, if you don't love yourself, how can you expect anyone else to love you?

Get the new you out and in circulation, make some new friends, go to some different places. All the old negative put down thoughts are now gone. You have become a success, and for successful people everything is possible. Never again say "I'm lousy at this" or "I couldn't do that." All things are now possible to YOU.

Imagine a basket full of beautiful apples and right on the top are several really rotten ones. Someone who sees the apples might say, "I don't want any of those, they're rotten!" You see, just one or two suspect fruit will spoil the whole lot.

Relate yourself to that. That lovely new self-image you have just planned for yourself will just not work if you don't give yourself the back-up and confidence necessary. Be sure there are no 'bad apples' in your self-image.

Start Your New Life

Now that the details have been sorted out and you can see everything clearly, it is time to start 'living' the new life. When you drive your car, feel as if you are driving a Rolls-Royce (if it's a Rolls you are after). Feel it purring along and attracting the attention of people on the pavement. They stop and look to see who it is driving that beautiful car. When you walk into a restaurant do it with the confidence of a movie star. I am not saying you should swagger and swank and be something you are not. Feel it inside. Feel it radiate out to touch everyone you see. But more of that later in the section on 'Charisma'.

The changes that are taking place in your self-image are happening within you, within your brain. As you command respect and success so you will get it. To begin with you will need to work at maintaining your self-image, but as the brain accepts that you are a success and you command respect, so it will become automatic. When that happens you will, quite naturally, be everything you planned and imagined.

Action

The key word is ACTION. Do it now; put your plans into action; do something, The time has come to stop talking and thinking about it, now it must be made to happen. Persevere and progress. Soon you will feel comfortable with your new self-image, as you would with a new pair of shoes. You will soon become accustomed to it and just like the image in the mirror, you will soon be able to love and respect it, because it really is YOU.

The difference at first between your old negative self-image and the new sparkling one may seem poles apart. Indeed, they should be, but the gap will narrow as the brain accepts that new image as real and eventually the gap will disappear completely as you and your new self-image become one and the same person.

This is not the end of the process by any means, because the situation is on-going. Now you will become successful and as successes pile up so your self-image will adjust accordingly, but now it will do it automatically without your having to instruct it. You will find that, quite naturally, bigger and more ambitious goals will become the norm. You will accept that anything you really want is possible and that YOU are capable of achieving it.

Your success will progress more quickly. In fact, you will tend not to look upon some of your achievements as successes – more, you will assume them to be normal. Which indeed they will be. More importantly, where your brain was keeping a file on all those negatives and failures, it is now listing positives and successes. Your future is looking good and you are feeling good. You are finding that people are relating to you in a more friendly and positive way. And with this progress the store of positive in the brain's pigeon-hole is growing fast, so now you will recall those successes and say with pride, "Did I do all that? Well, what do you know, I'm a success!"

Smile

This is something that works like a magic charm and never fails. Just a simple smile can add greatly to your whole self-image. Do you worry about what others think? Most people say they don't but deep down inside I'm sure they do. When they say "Oh I don't give a damn for anyone" it is just their ego talking. The truth is often the exact opposite: they do worry about their self-image but strangely many worry about how the other person sees them and not how they see themselves. How THEY would really like to be.

This misconception can be the cause of a poor self-image because you are working on the image you think someone else wants to see and not what YOU really want. If you want to lift your self-image in the eyes of others don't go out of your way too much. That could have false results and not be you at all. If you want to impress and give the impression that you are being very successful, reply with the biggest, broadest 'I-love-you' smile you can manage when you are asked, "How are you doing?" and simply say, "Just fine, thanks." Inject all the enthusiasm you can muster into it, then just keep quiet and watch the other person lift your self-image for you.

You'll marvel at the positive results. Used to best effect there is a great power in silence. A combination of silence and a smile can have a devastating effect. Try it.

You'll be able to hear their brain churning over as they think to themselves, "Hello, he's not telling me anything. He's on to something good and not saying anything. I bet he's making a lot of money."

It is the smile that does it. It is almost irresistible and works like a magnet. But remember, smile with the eyes and make eye-to-eye contact, it never fails. The smile coupled with the other person's imagination leads them to exaggerate and expand things out of all proportion. They will think that you have found the secret of hidden fortunes and all the while they are giving you a valuable free boost to the self-image.

A smile is like a new suit, it can make you feel really good because everyone will notice. It's a basic desire of every human being to want to be happy and the smile is the expression of that happiness and since everyone wants to be happy then that beautiful smile will act like a magnet. Try it and see.

Age

Some people, ever looking for excuses, often come up with the old chestnut, 'age'. It's a recurring problem and pure negative. They never seem to be happy with their present age. For some reason it always seems to be part of the reason 'why not'. "If only I was a bit older I'd have more credibility." "If only I had seen this opportunity ten years ago. . ." You will have heard these excuses; you may even have used them.

Please just forget about age, it simply does not matter. Thinking about it can do no good, because there is not a single thing anyone can do about it. It can cause very real setbacks. Remember, if you think you are too young to get a job or complete a task then you will fail because you are telling yourself this is so. That in itself is a slight on your self-image. 'You are what you think you are.' On the other hand, there is the person – definitely not to be encouraged – who thinks he or she is too old or 'past it'. That is as good as booking your own plot at the cemetery. Dangerous ground indeed. Too old, too young, it really does not matter, so don't let it become a problem.

I remember coming home from doing my two years' Military Service many years ago, when I was twenty-one. One of my brothers took me down to the pub for a pint, to celebrate. My brother, by the way, was only seventeen and under age to go into a pub.

He ordered two pints of ale and whilst the barmaid was 'pulling' them she nodded towards me and said to my brother, "Is he old enough to be in here?" We collapsed laughing, even though I found it flattering, but it could have meant a damaged ego to some people.

So why bother about age? What difference does it make? Why not turn it to advantage and say nothing, then who will know or doubt? Who wants to know anyway? Does it make any difference to you how old the people you deal with are? I doubt it very much. Life is fraught with enough problems as it is, don't look for more.

The next chapter looks at how to set about achieving your goals and dreams, and looks into the process that will bring them into reality for you.

Points from this chapter:

- Stop the rot
- Love yourself
- Change
- Build a new life
- You are the right age now

Chapter 3

Imaging

Creative Visualization

Have you ever noticed how successful people seem to attract even more success, without apparently even trying? They seem to be a magnet for success. Everything they do seems to turn to gold, seemingly without any effort. Success really does breed success and it is this very fact that is such a valuable asset. It is, in fact, one of the secrets of success. Because once you have seen some success, tasted the fruits of success and realized that you can achieve it, then you will be achieving it without thinking, exactly as it should be. And that is the very ingredients of successful imaging and success itself.

A Booster Shot

A field runner moving into the home stretch may feel exhausted and completely spent, but because his goal, the winning post, is in sight and he has another competitor on his tail, he finds that little extra help and energy. Just enough to make the difference between winning and loosing.

By the same token two football teams begin the match equal in every way. They play hard and struggle to score the first goal because once in the lead they know that that mysterious extra energy comes into play. That psychological boost really can be the deciding factor on the outcome of the game. In that situation you will often notice the trailing team fade, whilst the leaders harness that super extra energy or psychological advantage and draw yet further ahead.

That is just how you will work. Struggle, do whatever it takes to get within sight of those goals and as your success draws closer so will your self-confidence grow and the super extra energy become yours. One hard-fought success will hang the ladder down the mountain to help the rest clamber up. Then once this technique has been mastered you will have gained a valuable tool, the tool that helps success to breed success. You will then have at your disposal the very secret you have been searching for.

The Booster Shot Method

This is the first of two visualization concepts used in this chapter. I would suggest you use them both because both are very effective.

Here is the first simple process:

A. Set your goals.
B. Eat, sleep, and dream that goal. Give yourself and your brain instructions all the while – every detail, every how, what, why and when.
C. Then dismiss it from your mind completely and instruct the brain to 'get on with the job.' Just keep going in the direction of your goals.

At this stage your brain will begin acting for you, like the automatic pilot of a boat or aircraft. You have told it what to do, now just leave it alone to get on with the job. Have faith, do not interfere. Any intervention can only slow things down.

For example, if you were a taxi driver and you were instructed to drive a customer to the station, you would set off in complete control. You would know exactly where you were going and how you were going to get there. But if, suddenly, your customer sitting in the back, reached over and began turning the steering wheel, the result would be that you would not reach the station, but more likely crash your cab.

That is just how the brain works: tell it where you want to go and by what route, then simply let it take you there. Keep interfering and the journey will be delayed, if not terminated altogether.

That Gut Feeling

I must mention something very important at this stage. Something you will have experienced but maybe not have understood. And that is what is known as 'gut feeling'. Those unexplained instructions, urges, feelings (call them what you will) that instruct you to do, or not to do something. When you 'feel' that you should do something or go somewhere, but you just do not understand why, that can be an instruction from the brain, from your inner self. I cannot give a more scientific answer than that. Nevertheless take notice and act on it.

I don't think my faculties are any more advanced than average but when I get 'gut feelings' to do something, I do it without question. I have made some of the major decisions of my life in that way and with some very successful results. I am also not ashamed to say that I took one major decision against my 'gut feeling' which resulted in almost disastrous results. So watch out for them; they are very important and could change your whole life and even be worth millions to you.

How many times have you looked back at happenings in your past and said, "I had a feeling that would have been a good idea"? or "Something told me to do that but I didn't take any notice." It must have happened to everyone and simply because there was not a logical explanation it was not acted upon, and someone lost out as a result.

All you need to do is set your goals clearly and concisely then move into the action stage. Take notice of your 'feelings'. When you 'feel' it the right thing to do, or the right time to do it, then go ahead and put it into action. Do it! You are being guided by a greater force. Act on faith. Don't stop to worry about the whys and wherefores, just trust it, and act upon your intuition. You couldn't be in better hands.

Imagination

Imagination is a marvellous asset, common only to us humans. Just what it is, is difficult to say, because it is an intangible. It is not something that can be shared with another directly. We can't fill a jar with it, or see it, but we can share the results of its power, even though no one else can see or share what we see in our imagination. It is very powerful and often of overriding importance in the lives of so many people. It is the ultimate creative tool; it is in fact the act of creation, because every human achievement that has been made started in someone's imagination. Every single thing we do starts first with an image or picture, and that is created by the imagination.

In the previous chapter I talked about the self-image which is the all-important factor in success and achievement. All-important because what you see in your imagination, your mind's eye, is what you are, or what you get or attract. How many times have you hurt yourself, cut your fingers, say, and not until later when you have noticed the blood, does it begin to hurt? What happens is, the brain 'sees' blood and since blood and pain are associated, the message is flashed to the brain, 'Send down some hurt for this finger'. Then of course it does begin to hurt.

What curious magic is it that allows some people to be successful whilst others slave for a whole lifetime and never attain that ultimate state? What 'something' is it that separates winners from losers? A great friend of mine was an expert fisherman. He was amazing! If there were fish there, then Jack would catch 'em, and everyone who knew him was agreed about his prowess as a fisherman. As a boy, I recall fishing with him. He sat on one side of the boat and I on the other. Miraculously, Jack would catch fish whilst I, just two feet away on the other side of the boat, had not so much as a 'bite'.

"You must have the lucky side, Jack," I remember saying. Whereupon he handed me his line and took over mine. We simply changed places and as though some strange alchemy came into play, my original lines that Jack now held became alive beneath the hand of the master. And he caught fish, whilst I . . . well, you've guessed it!

What is this thing? My belief is that Jack's great reputation as a winning fisherman was in no doubt, but also my high regard for his ability made him even more effective. My effectiveness was made over to him by simply thinking "How could I be any match for the great Jack?" My image was not one of catching fish, it was an image of JACK catching fish, and therein lies the fundamental difference.

I am sure this same situation can be applied to just about everyone's success, and it is that other person's situation they image. You can get and achieve anything if you can clearly picture it in your mind. But the picture must be clear and crisp and in colour. Are the pictures in your mind clear? Most important of all, include yourself in those pictures. Try this test.

How Clearly do You See?

Close your eyes and visualize someone or something you know very well. It could be your wife or husband, your car or the garden from the window. Now, without cheating have a close look say at the garden. Is that tree in the garden really clear? Can you see exactly how the branches are shaped? And your wife – can you see her face in perfect detail? Do you really know what she looks like? Very few people can, because the mind requires only sufficient detail to establish who it is. The rest you assume.

One of the greatest reasons for failure is that people have the incorrect mental vision of what they really want, or what success is for them.

Sometimes what happens is that you set the correct mental images and get yourself on the road to success but before those first success images have been fulfilled you allow the other images to enter the picture, so the power generated by a single focused goal is weakened by additions and changes. Changing the whole goal amounts to the same thing.

Imagine making a cake. All the ingredients are mixed together and ready to cook in the oven. Halfway through the cooking you have a brainstorm and change your goal from that of a cake to that of bread, or some other goal. You throw in another set of ingredients and although they are the perfect recipe for your bread, together with the half-baked cake all you have is a mess, resembling neither a cake nor a loaf of bread. It is just an unsuccessful lump.

To be master of your own destiny requires finesse and determination. To be the skipper of your own ship you must know exactly what you want, where exactly you want to go, and not waiver for a moment in that desire and challenge. You must hold your course until the goal is reached.

Don't Change Boats in Mid-Channel

I recall a trip I made with my family across the English Channel in our boat *Solomon*. It was my first crossing as skipper and that made me a little apprehensive to begin with. I was confident about my navigation, yet after many hours out of sight of land, doubts arose. 'Am I right?' 'Am I going in the right direction?' Despite constant checking the doubts persisted. Hour after hour with nothing to do save check and recheck my navigation, brought about the doubts.

In mid-Channel we encountered many other small craft going in vaguely the same direction, but steering 10 degrees more westerly than we were.

"I think we should be going their way," said my wife Sue, with tongue in cheek.

"Where would they be going in that direction?" chipped in the kids, to add their doubt to the situation.

Sticking to my guns I insisted that we were on the correct course and that if I did alter it, then we would be lost! I was right to stick to my convictions, because we made our landfall right on target, although a little late. I entered the French port of Cherbourg proud to have arrived at my goal. The other craft we saw mid-Channel were heading for the Channel Islands. Just as with the analogy of baking the cake, had I altered course halfway across I too would have been in a mess.

Take command and hold those goals in your sights until you arrive. Be like a terrier with a rat – never let go, never give up. If something is wrong, face up to it squarely, now. If you need to change, then change NOW. DO IT NOW. Overcome these problems quickly, don't fool yourself. Most often the answer is work; get on and do it. I pulled a muscle in my back the other day and although it was very painful I had to keep going with what I was doing and I am sure my pulled muscle healed quicker than if I had succumbed and retired to bed feeling sorry for myself.

Dare To Think Success

We are slaves to our background and the only remedy that will lift us out of that inhibiting situation is the tion. Everything in your world revolves around how your how your life is now and has been in the past – the four walls encapsulating your very existence, and the only power strong enough to move those imprisoning walls is the imagination. Only by imagining something different can things be changed; without imagination the pattern will continue unaltererd. So 'dare' to imagine something better, something different, something new.

Images are the seeds of attainments. Nothing can be achieved or attained without first procuring the correct seed or image. If you plant lettuce seed in your garden you are not surprised to see little green lettuce leaves begin to shoot above the ground. You would be foolish to wait and see what's going to grow if nothing has been planted. So if images are the seeds of the things you want to achieve, you must clearly imagine what it is that you want. Be sure to image it as YOURS; include yourself in the visualization. It must be personal.

Accept that inside the framework of your body is another you, an infinitely more powerful, more profound being. It is the real you, it is your very soul. Somehow it is guarded, protected, shielded from the outward you. Often shielded to such a degree that many people are not aware of its existence. Some refuse to accept its existence but most intelligent people are aware that something at least exists. Often they do not know what it is, and even those rare souls who feel they do know, are often unable to acticulate or describe it adequately or with any credibility. So it remains unspoken or unwritten.

Who Knows?

I have no intention of delving into esoteric or para-psychological theories here, but I do feel justified in stating my opinions. For such subjects are not as yet accepted as the status quo, simply because scientific proof cannot yet be fully entertained. The refusal of the medical establishment to treat such theories with credibility makes difficult the task of assigning them as facts.

I have talked at some length with respected practitioners of psychology and each has reached their own conclusions which could be said to be fundamental and even indisputable but because of the 'state of the art' they must bite their tongues and say nothing. And for the same reason even the terminology has not been developed or established, so we have a situation where many may be talking about the same thing but calling it by different names. Often those names are more readily associated with the fiction of James Bond rather than the realities of modern science.

Hypnosis was such a subject until it gained respectability. Now it is a medical science. Well . . . almost, there are still pockets of resistance, but the facts can no longer be denied.

Acupuncture was another 'outlawed' science, but again it is emerging as an accepted practice. Perhaps not yet accepted in the truest sense, but gradually proving itself by results. People who cannot find a cure through orthodox medicine, turn in desperation to acupuncture and are overjoyed because it has worked for them. I know of many such cases. Sure, the sceptic may say that it worked simply because of its psychological effect on the patient, or the placebo effect. Maybe, but what does it matter so long as a cure or relief has been effected?

It seems to me that whilst people pioneer to research, rediscover and understand various psychological phenomena it is not until some bureaucratic body accepts the facts that these subjects become respectable. Until that time they are lumped together and labled as parapsychology, esoteric or mumbo-jumbo and brushed aside by the ruling fathers. Which I think is outrageous.

There is so much to learn in this wonderful machine we call the brain, that I would have thought that any research and information about its inner workings would be welcome. It is so complex and wonderful that, as yet, we can hardly even conceive of its potential, let alone know how it works. At this time only the smallest fraction of the human brain's potential has been tapped. I wonder what miracles there are within everyone of us, just waiting to be discovered?

On the subject of creating positive images I must make it clear that 'wishing' and 'hoping' are not the same as imaging. Wishing and hoping are fantasies of the uninformed and I ask you to draw the distinction. No matter how much you wish for something it is the precise image of the desire that will bring it about. We have no time for wishes, we are dealing only in positives, with goals and destinations.

One vital point it that once you have a clearly imaged or visualized goal then the more that image is kept in the mind's eye the better. For this reason I make no excuse for recalling the popular technique used in my book *How to be Rich and Successful* – that is, the magic of the red dot.

More Magic of the Red Dot

I advocated this method in a previous book and so popular has it become that I continue to recommend it because of its personal and positive advantages, and, more importantly, because it is so simple.

Since the brain can only respond to, and understand, pictures or images that is how your goals and dreams must be set. Once you have the mental 'picture' of your objectives stored away in the memory bank (your brain), then a method of recalling them is needed. Remember, the more you visualize those pictures the more you will want them to become real. The more obsessed you become towards achieving those pictures, the sooner you will achieve them.

What is needed is something to keep triggering your memory into throwing those precious pictures up on to that screen in your mind throughout each day. It is surprising, the kind of things that can recall a memory – a smell, a word, a song. In fact almost anything can trigger a trip down memory lane. The smell of chlorine, for me, instantly brings back the memories of swimming lessons at school and the music in the Ovaltine commercial on TV brings back whole streams of precious memories from the past. For others it may be the smell of the sea or the sight of a wedding, the smell of tar or the exciting scream of a jet plane.

Most people enjoy those impromptu trips back into the past but they do not always understand what brought them about. By using the magic of the red dot method ('red' springs to my mind, but any colour suitable to you may be used) you have complete control over what you recall and when. So it becomes a tool that can be used at your convenience. You can use this method to recall and bring back pictures YOU want whenever YOU want them. It really is very simple and most effective.

I use those sticky paper dots that peel off waxed sheets. The trick is to associate your thought picture with one of the coloured dots. Let's say your special goal is a beautiful new home, with circular driveway and pillars supporting the porch. Now see the picture of your lovely new home in your mind's eye, visualize it with a RED DOT hanging on the door, and never mentally see it again without it.

Armed with your sheet of red dots you can have instant recall whenever you need it. Put one on the dashboard of your car, on the inside of your wallet or purse, on your desk or machine at work or on the corner of the bathroom mirror. Now, wherever you see your red dot your mental success picture will come flooding back into your mind to give your self-motivation another jolt.

This method is really only a progression of the childhood practice of tying a knot in a hanky or putting a rubber band over your finger to remember something. In fact that system may suit you better but the advantage of the dots is that they can be placed strategically in positions that will 'jolt' your memory throughout the day.

Remember:

SEE IT – BELIEVE IT – ACHIEVE IT!

One sure way to keep faith in your pictures is to keep the picture bright and clear in your mind, and a sure way to do that is through the magic of the red dots.

Procrastination

As is well known, procrastination is one of the biggest 'bogy-men' of achievers – 'the thief of time' the more philosophical call it. It is one of the No No's we have all fallen foul of at some time or another. But sometimes although we know what has to be done and we keep saying to ourselves "I must get on with it" we still don't. There is a resistance, a something that holds us back. When this happens, and it happens to everyone, change your view of the goal. Look at things from another angle, have a fresh look. Try to breathe a new vitality into things. If your goal is a new car then go along to the garage for another 'booster' test drive.

Let's say, for example, your job takes you on a set route or to a set number of calls each week. There is little in it to stimulate you. You find the reason for disliking it; perhaps too much traffic on the route, lack of parking facilities and so on. Everything about it begins to irritate you. It becomes easy to find excuses for not going, or to cut corners. A very negative situation. The rot has set in.

What can be done? Try to find a positive approach, rebuild the challenges, replace the original goals and objectives with new images, new viewpoints. Visualize from a new angle, inject a new enthusiasm. Do whatever it takes to raise that energy level and to replace the spark of life. Then add ACTION to everything. Action is often the magic potion, the panacea that makes things begin to go right again. Get on your feet and into action and see for yourself the difference it makes.

We are ruled by the pictures or images within our brain. If they do not reflect your wishes there is a conflict of interest and it will not work. Understand that the brain is controlled by pictures, images, and not by spoken or written words. So to program it, obviously you must use pictures or images. It just will not respond to anything else. If you were to program a computer with the wrong computer language it just would not work, it simply would not understand the instructions. The same applies to the brain.

So if there are things that must be done, then the only way is to visualize them and to get them into their true perspective. To physically force yourself into work is not a productive situation. You can lead a horse to the water but you can't make him drink. An exciting visualization is the surest and quickest way. Use the magic tools at your disposal – imagination and enthusiasm – and watch out for the exciting results.

Imaging is not difficult with the help of the red dot.

Think

First, think. The thought is the miracle of creation. The thought comes first. The brain then has the amazing ability to produce a visual mental picture of that thought on demand. There is no other machine or devise on earth that can do that.

I have already said that if you are not yet the success you want to be then something has to be changed, otherwise everything will continue as before. I have also already said that you achieve things by imaging them and thinking about them. So if you have to change something you must change your thinking first, then your imaging. But my point here is that it is impossible to alter your thinking just like that. Here is the secret: before you can alter the way you think, you must first alter the way you see yourself, your self-image (see Chapter 2).

In the next chapter we look at a topic that determines your destiny, controls the result of everything you do. Positives and negatives, something everyone is aware of – but do they know how to control them?

Points from this chapter:

- 'GUT' feelings.
- Imagination.
- What makes winners?
- Dare to think success.
- More 'Red Dot' magic.
- Procrastination.

Chapter 4

The Power of the Positive

Are you sick and tired of being sick and tired? Are you sick and tired of being broke, of everything going wrong, of always missing the boat? Are you tired of being an 'also ran' instead of being the winner? If your answer is yes to any of those questions may I suggest that you read this chapter twice because the answer to your problem is here. It's a simple answer to a very common cause of failure.

The answer to this problem has been available to everyone since the ancient days of Solomon. It is well documented in the Bible. The answer has been right under your nose all the time. 'People often spend their whole lives looking for the key, only to find that it was already in the lock.' 'Howsoever ye speaketh, so will ye receive.' Or, if you want it straight in Dave Gannaway's English, "What you speak is what you get." That is the secret, the key; and the reason for so many failures is people's unawareness of this simple fact. It is just so simple people often miss it. People often find it difficult to do simple things.

What Problem?

One of the biggest problems with overcoming a negative attitude is that people do not realize they have a problem to begin with. Like the person who has B.O.: that person is always the last to know the problem because he is used to smelling like that. He knows no difference. He will be unaware that the reason people are holding their noses is HIM.

That's a curious fact but often true. It is also true that a positive and a negative attitude also attracts or repels each other, like to like. Negative people are naturally drawn and attracted to negative people and repel and rebel against the positive. Even though they understand what is right their deep-rooted negative attitude will not allow them to think any other way.

What is Negative?

Many people simply do not know that they are being negative. All too often they criticize others for being negative when in fact they are every bit as bad. If you say "Oh, I just can't do anything right these days," then I guarantee that is exactly what will happen. Everything will go wrong. It is sure to go wrong because you have programmed your brain for everything to go wrong.

How many times have you heard people say, "Oh I do feel ill." Sure they do, and by saying and believing it they have programmed those facts into the brain. I was listening to two ladies talking the other day and one said, holding her jaw, "I'm going to have trouble with this tooth, I just know it." Guess what? Within a short while it became so painful that she insisted it be removed. And just before she went in for the extraction she was saying, "Every time I have a tooth out I get an abscess in the gum." You guessed it, she did. In fact she was a negative walking disaster.

What you say is what you get. You actually create your own future by what you say and believe. The brain is a miracle, it alone can make you a success. But it works on what it is fed, so if you, as its keeper, feed it negatives and junk, that is exactly what you will receive. So when you say "Oh I can't do that," what you are telling your brain is that it can't be done and, just as you would expect, it won't be.

Attitudes

It is your mental attitude that determines how you act and react to the challenges of everyday life. Quite simply, if you have command of a positive mental attitude you will be a success. A negative mental attitude produces failure. It is really as simple as that.

Some people are aware of that fact, others are not. Some are naive about this and will be enlightened by this chapter, others will read it and conclude that it does not apply to them. Many, although fully aware of the problem, may find it difficult to make any impression on a well-established negative attitude.

There is a natural magnetism between positive people and once you have learned the very substantial advantages of keeping the mind positive the mechanics will quickly follow. Like so many other things connected with self-motivation and self-improvement the main requirement is the formation of a new habit.

Alter your disposition. Change your route through life. Take the happiness road – it's fun, it's bright, the company's just terrific and the end of the road is success. The bonus to that success is that you made many friends on the way and enjoyed every minute of the trip. Follow the crowd and you will lead the life of a sheep, being herded from pillar to post. Hounded by the shepherd's dog, ruled by his whistle and destined to satisfy someone else's appetite.

Why do people act like sheep? I guess they feel safe in numbers, in a herd. If just one of them could get smart enough, he could realize that by changing he could become head of that pack. All it needs is to think for yourself, break away and do your own thing. All that is needed is to say "Hey! I'm not going that way, things look better my way", and DO IT.

Doing just that will lift you out of that flock and make you a potential leader. The rest of the sheep may look and say, "Hang-on! He may be right, it might be better his way, come on fellers, let's follow him." Then you *are* the leader. By making that simple change you could find yourself head of the pack, the leader, the boss, or whatever you want to be.

You can 'turn the tables'. So wake up, for goodness sake. Look about you at all those silly sheep running around getting nowhere. Wise-up now and think positive. See what the masses are doing and do the opposite. Be your own man, the master of your own destiny.

Look for the Good

A person who has a negative attitude is always looking for the bad in people and things. He looks for what is wrong and what is going to go wrong. He puts himself down and puts everyone else down also. He finds it difficult to love anyone and more importantly can't love himself. This leads back to negative self-image (see Chapter 2). So ingrained can the negative gloom become that its practitioners become addicted to it. They actually do things expecting to fail. Can you believe that? It's true. I know people personally who enjoy, genuinely enjoy, being miserable. I'm sure you must know folk like that too.

I find it amazing how pathetically unhappy some people are. There have been times when I have tried to help, and I mean really tried, but I failed simply because the person concerned could not break the habit of thinking failure. So convinced were they that nothing, but nothing, would change their view that what they were left with, a straight nothing, was what fate had planned for them. What God intended will be. If you know people like that try to get through to them that GOD never put anything or anyone on this earth to fail, and they are no exception.

Recycle 'em

Look upon negative materials and attitudes as faulty positives that need adjusting. Find what is wrong with them, correct them, then put them back to work – this time as positives – recycle 'em. Understand that anything negative is potentially destructive, so handle with care. Like a doctor dealing with a patient with a contagious disease. Take every precaution, but make it your business to cure that disease and set things right.

For example, if you had a friend who snubbed you or upset you in some way, the negative reaction would be for you yourself to get upset and retaliate – "Right, you son-of-a-bitch, you'll pay for that. . . ." Fighting fire with fire may give vent to your feelings in the short term, but it is totally the wrong approach. Try to understand that something must have upset your friend to act that way. ". . . That's unlike him to behave like that, something must be bothering him. . . ." That is a far more positive and constructive attitude.

Here's another example. When my two sons were small I remember they had several different sets of building bricks all mixed in together, some of stronger composition than the others. In one of the sets were small replicas of house bricks. They were red and made of soft rubber. Everyone has seen a child's building blocks, with which, together with their wonderful imagination, they can make anything from ships to castles.

As I watched one day, they built a beautiful castle, with all the soft red rubber bricks on the bottom, and as the castle walls grew so the red bricks on the bottom began to collapse under the weight of the heavier blocks. Then, because the few red rubber bricks on the bottom caved in, so the whole beautiful castle trembled and fell into a heap.

I thought my sons were pretty smart for, as I watched in wonderment they rebuilt the castle, but this time without using the red bricks at the base, and guess what? – the castle never toppled any more. And that illustrates my point nicely. Those red blocks are the same as the negatives and weaknesses in your make-up. What you need to do is 'leave them out', know which is your 'red blocks', re-cycle them, change them, substitute them for something that will bring more positive results. If you know what you are doing wrong, then stop doing it NOW.

Negative Spotter

How do you identify a negative person from a positive person? One obvious pointer is the negative person is a professional fault-finder. He will meet a person and look for the negative, the faults; he is also always suspicious. You will notice that he will often give you a sideways glance of distrust. Even if that person tries to extend the hand of friendship his negative attitude will spoil the relationship. But if that does happen, do not retaliate with aggression or try to compete with his negative ways. You will win the day if you stick to your guns and be positive and leave the situation with a smile.

Imagine a friend stops by to invite a negative person to dinner; maybe he is new in the neighbourhood and wants to offer his friendship. The negative guy's response will be, "Oh, yes, he's only inviting me over to prove that he's got more than we have." Or, "Oh, he must want to borrow something!" I bet you have met someone like that too.

The positive person looks for the good in people. He may meet a real villain but his response will be, "I don't know what Joe's done but he is real fun to be with." So there is the basic difference. How do you identify with it? Don't be afraid to admit that one or two of those examples hit a nerve. Everyone has been negative to some degree at some time. We live in a very negative world. Just understand that you can change, and believe me it is so much more fun to be positive, to see the good things that are all about you rather than all the bad. Stop being a sheep following the negative majority. Break away from that 95% of the population who are losers. Outweigh negative with positive. Form a habit to use the positive to flush away the negative. Understand that positive people are winners. Positive people are happy people and just everyone wants to be happy.

Doctor, Doctor!

How would you respond if you were in hospital to undergo an operation and the surgeon arrived at your bedside sporting two bloodshot eyes and an ice-pack on his head, obviously nursing a hangover. If he said, "Oh, I do feel ill . . . never again . . . I can't stop trembling . . ." you would not have too much faith in his making a success of the operation, would you?

A silly example, of course, but by the same token if you spend your opportunities moping about saying that you can't do this or can't do that, that is exactly how it will be. You'll not do anything. So it will hardly be surprising that opportunities will not be extended to you nor will you gain any credibility and confidence.

The negative person is one who has an excuse for everything. A permanent reason for not doing this and not doing that. The world is full of them.

The Positive Plus

What are some of the advantages of life with a positive mental attitude?

A positive mental attitude:

1. Attracts good and positive things.
2. Attracts wealth and happiness.
3. Attracts successful people.
4. Attracts your life's goals and dreams.
5. Will lift your whole life on to a new and successful plane. And much, much more.

Understanding and learning the way of the positive are just the beginning of the success process. The benefits and success themselves come when the understanding and learning are applied to your life. When you turn them into action. There would be little point in installing a doorbell if you didn't intend to open the door when someone rang.

The magic of the positive is something that everyone has, yet few bother to use. It is free; now that you are aware of it you can control your own destiny. You are free to use it as you will. You can use it to free yourself of all that negativeness of the past. There is not another living soul on this earth exactly like you. You are unique. You have powers that make us one-offs in the animal kingdom. Learn those powers and use them to improve your life.

Positive Attitudes

A positive attitude is synonymous with success. It is the cornerstone upon which success in all its many guises is built. People who succeed are aware of this and don't need to be told, but there are a lot of people around who have not yet learned the lesson.

I've heard people say, "Oh, don't give me all that positive thinking garbage, it doesn't work." Sure it doesn't work for them, but only because they don't want it to work. Anyone can spot the things that don't work, that requires no effort at all. And those are likely to be the same persons who try once and fail and never try again. In a word, they are losers. That is the only way to describe them. And frankly their losing, negative attitudes radiate like a pea-soup fog and are inclined to embrace us all with it. "If I can't do it – neither can you," they say, setting themselves up as both judge and jury.

Find the Hot Button

Once you learn to see the tremendous value of understanding and using the power of the positive attitude you have a wonderful and invaluable philosophy at your disposal.

Most people will agree that when they are 'full of beans', enthusiastic, feeling ten feet tall and confident, everything good seems to happen. For some reason everything goes right. Opportunities crop up, you meet people, your luck just seems to be in. You feel good about yourself, just everything seems to have a rosy complexion. The reason is the power of the positive. YOU plus this wonderful positive charge make that magic.

You are, I'm sure, aware of it when it happens but do you know 'what' makes it happen? Do you understand the sequence of events that produces that 'high' state? From this moment in time make it your business to know. If something gives you that extra boost of enthusiasm, know and understand what that something is. Because until now you are only able to take advantage and use that super-boost when 'IT' decides to show itself. But if you find what 'IT' is, then you can learn to turn it on when you need it and that has very obvious advantages.

For myself I have spent a little effort in understanding these things. Now I like to think that I have control over most situations, simply by bothering to find out what the positive hot button was for me. If I need to create a favourable impression that requires me being the best 'me' I can possibly muster, then I know what to do. I can now guarantee that I am in peak psychological condition just when I need to be.

There is nothing magic about it. Simply take the time to understand what turns you on, what is your positive hot button and how to use it. It is every bit as important as how you look and dress, because if you have a high mental feeling you will have 'presence' or 'charisma'. A quality so many envy yet cannot achieve.

The True Secret of Success

Every book dealing with self-help and motivational topics boasts a 'secret'. The secret of success, the secret of personal magnetism, the secret of the perfect memory, etc., and those secrets do, I am sure, hold the truth of that success. But there is one secret above all you should understand if you are to find advantage in any motivational reading and that secret is to have a genuine, desperate desire to achieve those goals or improvements.

The key to all success is ACTION – DOING it. How to do it and when can be learnt from a teacher or from books but all the books in the world or the very best of teachers can't give you skill and mastery over your subject. You alone have to achieve that. Instruction can lead in the right direction but only one thing can give you that skill you require, and that is action. You must get up, get out, and do it for yourself.

Possibly the first time you do it may prove to be a disappointment, but persistence, imagination and real desire for success will assure positive results. If you love doing what you want to do and are dedicated to success, then success is guaranteed. You will come to terms with any problems or obstacles that may arise and you will ultimately triumph. 'Out of every adversary lies the seeds of a bigger and better benefit.' Learn it, then DO IT. ACTION is the key word.

About Reading

For many, reading is an unnecessary chore or one that must be tackled and completed as quickly as possible. That is fine if you want only the 'gist' of what the author has to say. If you want maximum information, absorption of the written word is necessary and should be undertaken more methodically. For example, if you attend an instructional talk or lecture it is standard practice for the speaker to first introduce the topics and areas to be covered, state the broad concept or the bare bones of the talk. Then he will return to the beginning and talk about each stage or topic in turn. Moving along stage by stage, taking time to think, to analyse and digest.

This is how the serious reader should approach a book

of this type. Read it through to begin with to understand what the author is dealing with. Then return to the beginning. The method I use works very well, I keep a marker pen by me whilst I read, then each time I come across a passage I may wish to refer back to, I mark it. This provides a quick and easy reference, although it does mess up the book for anyone else. Another way is to buy two books and cut out the sections that are important to you from one book and save in a Resource file leaving the other copy intact. So, naturally, this method is recommended only for your own books. But it does allow quick reference and access to important information.

Another point is that as you develop and stretch so your understanding and viewpoint change. So I find it invaluable to re-read the book, again and again, and each time I find something new and obtain a greater understanding of it. After all, as I have said before, if you are not already rich and successful then there is something 'not quite right' with your technique, something that needs changing and it is by forming new habits and repeated reference to the instructional material that will ensure it.

How does a concert pianist become so accomplished? By constant practice and a deep desire to achieve the goal; ACTION is the simple answer. He may be able to read the music and play the score on sight very quickly, but to reproduce the magic and interpret it as the composer intended, the musician needs to study, practise and understand. Just like you. You have all the requirements, so just add ACTION and you will be the maestro of your own SUCCESS.

Caution

To recommend that caution be thrown to the wind would be silly. Also, life without basic caution would probably see you run over the first time you crossed the street, burn yourself when you made yourself a coffee, or even fall off the chair when you stood on it to clean the windows. There will always be those characters who will fall down that hole however well marked it is and will step on that upturned rake so that the handle will spring up and give them a nasty knock. They will always be there.

But excess caution in business is another matter. If not directed properly it will restrict your growth and progress by always shrouding things in a protective coat. The businessman too can lose that 'snap' if the component of risk, the buccaneer element of danger is removed. Personal performance is, in fact, normally enhanced by cultivating a more daring or more extrovert attitude. A British Army division noted for its specialist daring, has the motto 'Who Dares Wins', and that is so true. So dare to be more imaginative, a little more devil-may-care. You may find it will bring to the fore exciting elements of your character that you were unaware of.

For the person who will not or cannot take a risk, who needs security, who wants a guarantee that next week's wages will be waiting, my advice is to get an ordinary job, because the true 'have-a-go' attitude will not flourish with the restriction imposed by too much caution. You can never know what you can do until you try. Most people amaze themselves at the abilities that come to the forefront when they place themselves in a position where they have to pull out all the stops, where they have to win to survive.

Success in Sight

When success is in your sights, when you get the 'bit' between your teeth, you will settle for nothing but those targets you were aiming for. It does not matter what it takes, what problems need to be overcome. You are heading for your goals and cheerfully accept whatever is required of yourself. Obstacles great or small make little difference if your desire to succeed is desperate enough.

There are no assurances, no guarantees. Be it smooth or bumpy the road to success has to be travelled without cutting corners, there is no other way. Over mountains or deserts, it does not matter. You will do whatever needs to be done and keep on until success is in the bag.

How do you know what it takes? You don't. How do you know what is over the next hill or round the next bend in the road? You don't. Around the next bend could be your treasured success or it could be yet another bend, another bumpy road. Never mind, don't let it get you down, keep on going and doing what needs to be done. When you think about it, there is nothing else you can do. To keep on going is the only option left open to you. If you are a winner you can't give up, so the only thing to do is to square those shoulders and keep right on going.

The Way to be Safe . . .

My own personal motto is 'The way to be safe is never to be secure', and it has always worked for me. In fact those times of my life when I have been secure have also been the most negative and unproductive. From time to time I am asked for my advice on various schemes and ideas; it is very flattering and very often the ideas are worthy of being taken up. But strangely I feel that the people who ask know that already, they know a good idea when it is pointed out to them, and what is required of me is to give them assurance, confidence or whatever, enough to put the idea into practice. Sadly, all too often the projects become so scrutinized by negative points of view that the whole thing fades from view before their very eyes. Like a beautiful rose being picked before it has a chance to bloom and become a thing of beauty.

I was once shown a clever idea concerning a household product by a very smart young man. I had no doubt that it would have been a success. My advice was to 'get cracking', get on with it, produce the item.

"Yes, but if only I could be sure people would buy it . . ." If only . . . How many times have those two little words stood in the way of a fortune! You see caution, in this instance, is sounding the death knell on that idea. He wants the success without the risk and that just does not work. So that is why success makes successful people special.

With business you must be prepared to 'put your money where your mouth is', or 'to put the required time commitment and effort in.' If you have an idea, you need to stand by it yourself. Most every business needs an investment of some form at the beginning; it may be in the form of cash or time and effort. Nothing is for nothing, there is no such thing as a 'free lunch' so you will never know just how good that idea or product is until you can display the finished article. Failure to do that means that you have not got complete confidence in your own idea, you are negative about it.

Often I have talked to people about business ideas and concepts, and in most cases they would dearly love to have a business of their own, but caution holds them back. I have even offered people the opportunity to own their own business, with no capital required, only a little of their spare time, and it is surprising how many even hesitate at that!

A friend of mine, author Scott Alexander, says, "You should have the audacity of the Rhino, and 'charge' your way towards your goals." How true that is and I am sure rhinos never give a second thought to caution!

The Wildcatter's Secret

If you read accounts of how the professional entrepreneur works, this one quality comes to light in almost every case. When something 'feels' right, when that 'gut feeling' tells them O.K., then there's no hesitation. Like the rhino they put their head down and charge, they go for it no matter what. Anything in the way either gets trodden on or overcome in whatever way possible.

Once they feel right then they 'have a go'. Without thought of risk, we'll face our problems when we come to them, they say. Complete confidence that everything will turn out for the best is the order of the day, and the recipe for success.

The late J. Paul Getty speculated millions. He put his shirt on the oil rights to a piece of land that had no evidence of the presence of oil. Nor had any land for miles around ever produced a single drop of oil, yet he played his 'gut feeling' and it paid off. He made another king's ransom.

Most businessmen of this type make their money in this way. They are go-getters in the extreme. Often with little or no knowledge of the finer points of a project they will charge in with guns blazing and pull off amazing deals. Often it is a win all, lose all situation, a commercial Russian roulette.

Can you imagine Paul Getty approaching the owner of that prospective drilling sight and saying, "Let me drill a trial well. If there is oil there, then I'll buy the land, but if it turns out to be dry then we'll forget it." Too silly, isn't it? But that is what a lot of cautious people would like to do.

What would Mr Getty do? My guess is that he would hire someone, probably a lesser-known negotiator, to negotiate and purchase the land at the cheapest possible rate, since he would understand that the very mention of his name would send the price soaring.

Start to be smart and understand that over 90% of the population never achieve their goals, they are losers, so it makes a lot of sense to find out what the majority are doing in their effort to be successful, and then for you to DO THE OPPOSITE. Stop following the leader because there is a 9 to 1 chance that he will fail and fall flat on his face.

Danger! Epidemic!

At all costs keep yourself from exposure to the negative. Unlike with contagious diseases it is not possible to take a pill three times a day, and put everything to rights. Nor can you isolate yourself from the world of the negative, simply because the majority of the world IS negative.

When I was a lad I loved to paint pictures with water colours. My Mum would give me a glass of crystal clear water to wash my brush in and it never failed to fascinate me how even the smallest amount of paint would colour the whole glass of water.

Negative people are like that. Just one can make the whole community around him negative. For some reason better known to themselves, people seem to be attracted more readily to the negative than to the positive. Maybe it is easier to be negative and follow like sheep. Maybe the thought of striving for success with the work and effort involved is too much for some to come to terms with. It can also be fear, fear of failure or fear of success. Both are very real problems. Who knows? It's little wonder that most of our population is thoroughly negative.

Negative thinking spreads like the plague. Already it is at epidemic proportions, it is running rife, heading its victims towards that downward spiral that leads to more and more negatives. So take every precaution you can against becoming yet another victim. You can prevent it simply by refusing to listen to all that negative 'tripe'. When someone next starts one of those monotonous monologues of doom and destruction let it ring a bell in your brain – 'danger', 'danger'. Move away, excuse yourself or simply say, "I'm sorry, but I'm just not going to listen to all this negative garbage any longer." You will be respected for it and when you see that person next you can be sure you'll not hear him being negative in front of you. It may even bring home to him the error of his ways! But whatever happens, surround yourself with positive people and you will feel safe and more at home. Outweigh all those negatives with positives.

In the next chapter I am going to deal with an idea that everyone employs but often without realizing it. Duplication is a topic rarely discussed in the pages of motivational books, yet used with common sense it can be the short-cut to the success you are searching for.

Points from this chapter:

- The power of the positive.
- Attitudes.
- What is negative.
- The wildcatter's secret.
- Add action for success.
- Find your hot button.
- About reading.
- The true secret of success.

Chapter 5

Duplication

Duplication is not a topic that often appears within the pages of a motivational book. The meaning of the word 'duplication' is quite straightforward, it means 'by example', 'exactly alike' or 'to multiply by example'. For those who dare to succeed, duplication is a word that should be fully understood because it can provide the obvious doorway to the halls of success and can save a great deal of time and trouble along the way.

Many folk start out on the road to success with everything in its correct order, and yet still fail. They have beautiful goals and dreams, they have enthusiasm, a good self-image, in fact everything is as it should be, but still success eludes them. Search as they may something is missing, something is preventing a breakthrough.

So what is it and how can duplication help? Well, in a nutshell it simply amounts to following a plan that has already proven to be successful. For example, if your father ran a successful business then it would be foolish not to seek his advice and to duplicate his proven plan. All the problems he has overcome and valuable lessons he has learned over the years could be passed to you direct, saving months, even years, of learning the hard way. In terms of money too the saving could be immense. So why start at the beginning when you can be off to a flying start by duplicating an already successful plan?

Your goal may be to rise to a high managerial position in the company you work for or it may be to become an expert at some skill or craft. Duplication works in all situations. As I have mentioned before, my son has become a pilot and he has done so by duplicating a proven successful plan built up by those pilots who have trodden that route successfully before him.

For others the goal may be wealth or financial freedom – then they need a business of their own. Whatever your goals and whatever success is for you by understanding the process of duplication your path ahead can be cleared of many obstacles and potential hazards. Naturally all the pitfalls may not be illuminated, but duplication could just make the difference between success and failure.

Compare

To draw a comparison, think of the success process as a motor-car journey. The destination is your goal, the car is the business vehicle. Success requires five basic ingredients and they apply to any business, be it a giant multi-million pound company or a one-man corner grocery store. Success will not come if any of the five ingredients are missing.

Let us then look and compare them with our motor-car journey.

1. Goals and dreams. = The destination of the car.
2. A business of your own. = The vehicle.
3. Enthusiasm and motivation. = The fuel.
4. Your desperate desire to win. = The driver.
5. Know-how. = Know-how.

Let's look in a little more detail:

1. DREAM = DESTINATION

Before any trip can be made, you must first know exactly where you want to go, your destination – the object of your ambitions, goals and dreams. You must also know where you are setting out from. There would be little point in trying to plan your route on the road map if you did not know where you were starting from.

2. BUSINESS = VEHICLE

A journey is not possible unless there is a vehicle to take you where you wish to go – a business of your own with potential enough to finance your achievements. But don't choose a business exactly to size because you will want to expand and stretch as your success grows.

3. ENTHUSIASM = FUEL

The vehicle will not work without fuel. The main fuel that a business requires is enthusiasm and motivation, the very life-blood of a business. Again, even if you know what fuel to use you must also know where to get it when it is needed. What to do and how to motivate yourself when required to do it.

4. DESIRE = DRIVER

A vehicle requires a driver. YOU are the driver, you know where you are heading and are prepared to do what it takes. Remember, dreams and opportunities often present themselves after hours; if you have locked doors for the night, you could miss them. Always be ready to move on. Keep your mind open, keep the engine running. To have a closed mind is like putting the car into the garage and shutting the door. It will do nothing but gather dust. So have the car out, tank topped-up and be ready for anything exciting that happens to come by. Many opportunities bloom from a chance action or meeting. A casual word even a smile, can be the beginning of something great. Always be ready.

5. KNOW-HOW = KNOW-HOW

To bring all these things together requires the know-how, information, and experience. For starters, the driver will need to learn how to control the car, what fuel to get and where to get it and to be able to read a map that will show him the direction of his destination. Have enough faith in yourself to know that you can do it. It could be that some of the information that you require other people have worked a lifetime to accumulate. If that is the case then ask, Be big enough to understand that and admit it. If you learn to approach this type of challenge with a positive attitude, the information will be forthcoming without any problem. (Proper attitude is a vital factor in the struggle for success. See Chapter 7.)

In this chapter I shall be dealing with this last item, No. 5 – Know-how, Information and Experience: all qualities that are gathered through the process of achieving and succeeding, often over many years. Stored experiences and a million and one snippits of information, all filed away and on tap in the owner's brain.

The only problem is that if you are young and starting out in life your own store of this wisdom has not yet been developed. Or you may be starting a project which is entirely new. So how, I hear you ask, can I obtain that knowledge? "I can't wait for ever to collect that information for myself, I'm in a hurry, hungry for those goals now."

The answer I am going to give you is so simple that you will kick yourself for not spotting it. Why don't you simply ASK HOW. Why not let someone 'SHOW YOU' what to do? It is so simple, isn't it? Why do people try to invent the wheel when it has already been invented. All you need to do is find someone with the information you want and ask. Should you be rebuffed, don't worry – look, watch, and listen, then try it anyway.

You can if you try

Many years ago I applied for a position in a highly complex project. When I went for the appointment I knew that it would stretch my ability to the very limit and it did. In fact, the job proved to be even more demanding than I had imagined. So precise and exacting was the work that I decided to 'come clean' and admit that I was getting out of my depth.

I talked it over with the boss and, incredibly, he said I'd be silly to quit because he was sure that I COULD do the work. From that moment on he gave me all the help I could possibly want. He really went the extra mile to help me over that situation.

Winners find a Way

Another of my own personal rules is quite simple: winners find a way, so if I can't go in the front door, I go around to the back door. If I can't get over the fence, then I will go under it. When I have this great urge to do something,

NOTHING that is within the law will stop me. Be like that, go for it!

Don't Counsel with Fools

Now, see what happens so often when people start out on the road to success: they look around for advice, they are hungry to learn the secrets of success, the way to make money. So hungry in fact that they ask advice of anyone: friends, family, anyone who will talk on the subject. It is very flattering to be asked for advice, so even a fool when asked his advice will give it. Good or bad the advice starts to flow freely, just about everyone has something to say on your subject. Well that is just fine, provided that the people who are giving the advice are worthy of giving it – that they have fruit on their tree and are successful themselves. Because if they are not (not wishing to be unkind), it is a case of the blind leading the blind.

How can anyone offer you advice on, for instance, how to make money if they are broke themselves? Otherwise, why did they not follow their own advice? If you wanted to be a doctor you wouldn't seek advice from a carpenter. You may think that is a silly example, but it is even more silly to ask a failure how to make money. Yet that is what happens and it happens amazingly often. No, the only way to learn success is from someone who is a success. I'm sure that makes much more sense.

This is not a contradiction, it is the truth – good advice is not easy to come by. Few people get the opportunity to get the right kind of advice simply because they go to the wrong source.

Consider this example: Let's say your are planning to set yourself up in a small grocery business. In the process of 'looking' you get into conversation with the owner of a grocery store who, just by chance, has such a business for sale. By listening to his glowing narrative on grocery shops, how profitable they can be, etc., you could be misled, unless you asked yourself the question, "If his grocery shop is so successful then why is he selling it?"

This type of businessman plays his cards very close to his chest. Oh he will tell you how loyal he is and that he is 'honest to a fault'. But I doubt if this type of character could or would show you the profits on a set of accounts.

There will be other businessmen who will of course be of the highest integrity and the most genuine people you could meet. But so often when you look they have no apples on their tree, they have little achievements to show for their 'vast experience', AND wealth of knowledge.

Duplicating a Profession

Let's have a look at what happens when someone takes to a trade or some highly skilled profession. Take a craft such as my own, boatbuilding. When a young man enters the boatyard gates he is set to work under the wing of an experienced craftsman. To begin with, he just watches, fetches and carries, because that is the limit of his abilities. But slowly he learns to use tools, all under the watchful eye of the master.

He is shown, he duplicates, he is shown again. He learns to handle the tools, saw in a straight line, drill a hole square, to identify different types and qualities of timbers. Little by little he absorbs the treasure of knowledge that is being fed to him. The apprentice sees time and time again how the craftsman produces his beautiful work. He learns what to do and how to do it. He is set standards to maintain. All the while he is growing in his abilities as a craftsman and his understanding of the world into which he is becoming a part.

Time is part of the process, he is absorbing the dust of ages, the skills, knowledge, even memories and stories. Everything he will need to become a duplication, the image, of his craftsman mate. In fact the whole way of life. He learns to savour the very life's blood of the craft he has chosen, even how to think like a boatbuilder.

He will learn to see beauty in new things; in timber, in the curves and lines that make a boat, in the razor sharp 'sing' of a shaving curling from a plane, and the unforgettable smell of teak or pitch pine. Those words bring the memories flooding back.

The method of duplication has transferred the benefits and treasures of another person's whole lifetime of experience. In this way the craft evolves and progresses. Without the love and true desire to procreate the craft through this duplication process, or if experienced craftsmen declined to pass on their skills, the crafts would die. A good example of this is the wheelwright, cooper and thatcher and many more.

It is interesting to see that just a few of these wonderful skills and crafts are in fact being saved from extinction by a handful of the craftsmen who 'hurt' to feel their craft dying. Their goals and dreams become just that – to pass it on and save it from extinction.

The tide is turning. Demand for beautiful things will always return because beauty changes with fashion. A hand-crafted boat is a heart-warming sight that draws attention from everyone who understands quality and skill. There will always be a future for such craftsmen provided they can supplement their skills with a little entrepreneurial flare.

Craftsmen able to repair, replace, rebuild or even duplicate such treasures will enjoy an increase in demand. They will acquire all the work they need and earn a fine living if they let their commercial skills grow with the twentieth century whilst maintaining their traditional skills. Once they understand that those skills are rare and that the people of wealth who want something special will pay handsomely, then they will realize their true value. How many people, I wonder, reading these words have such skills yet cannot see the potential? Many, I feel sure, will say, "The old trade is dead and gone, let it rest in peace." But for the craftsmen who are not 'quitters' they will discover theirs is a gift that could be worth a fortune. (Thatchers, for instance, have now become so sought-after that their services are booked a year or two ahead.)

Duplicate the New

Duplication on a more commercial basis is clearly illustrated when considering some of the modern chain stores and supermarkets. They develop in a far more financially oriented way than smaller operators. To begin with, these operators, or investors, build and open a single store. They then go to whatever lengths it takes to make it profitable. They formulate how many check-outs and what staff will be required, they plan layout and stock-levels and every other detail that determines the success of such an establishment. Even the type of people they want to attract. Then, when the first single business is open and running at a profit, and all the snags and hiccups have been ironed out, it becomes simply a matter of duplication to increase the business volume and profits. For that reason you will notice that throughout the chain each store is exactly the same as the first. That first success is duplicated over and over again. Basically, it really is sound common sense.

The managers and staff of each new store are taught the methods from managers and staff of the successful store. Any developments, improvements or time-saving methods are all incorporated in the teaching of the new staff. That is duplication at work and remember, even the largest supermarket chain started with a single link!

The staff of the new store need not bother about research and learning by mistakes, the lessons have already been learned once. Think what a slow and time-wasting process it would be if each new store had to start back at the beginning and learn by its own mistakes!

Personal growth is like that. If you want to open up your own business, be it that corner shop or a multi-level marketing organization, would it not make good sense to search out someone who has already been successful in that sphere? And provided there is no financial threat to them, and you are not going to be a cause of 'hassle', successful people are normally only too pleased to be asked to help. Try it, what have you to lose?

Duplicate Quick-Start

I often wonder why most individuals look for their start in poverty and hardship. As though by some basic instinct some people, particularly the young, have the perverse idea that the route to success must start at the poverty end. As though it is mandatory to rise through poverty. To spend the first part of their lives struggling in statutory ignorance and poverty whilst the first lesson runs its course.

Naturally everyone must start at the beginning. Every journey starts with a single step. But start that journey from where you are right now, today. Ask and listen to those you can see have done it. Then, most important of all, DO IT. By just following that simple instruction the rise to success could be made much easier and quicker. COME ON! LET'S GO!

Get Down to Details

We have looked at duplication as a broad picture, now let us 'home in' on some of the details. Let us imagine you are just starting in business. You know that a bank account will be essential but you have never had any dealings with a bank, in fact in all probability you don't even have an account or have any idea how the banking system works.

So the obvious first – a trip to the bank. If you select one of the larger High Street branches, there will probably be a separate little table with a personal assistant all ready to help. Ask for all the information you require. You will find the bank staff will be delighted to help in any way, because you are a potential customer. The information you get will be straight from the horse's mouth.

If you want to know how the bank works from the businessman's point of view – you got it, ask a businessman. A little spade work in this area can be of great help to you. Provided you make contact with the right person to begin with, the information you could end up with could be invaluable. If he is successful and you duplicate what he says, guess what? You will be successful too. People love to help, but they can't read your mind, you must first ask. There is no harm in asking: if you don't ask, you don't get.

Success breeds success. If you associate with successful people then you will become successful. Adopt the methods I have just described and watch what happens. You will begin to make contacts and develop associations with winners. Things happen when you put yourself into the correct situations. Opportunities will open up for you as the result of just associating with the type of people you want to emulate. Mix with winners and you will become a winner – it never fails.

Duplication is in every-day use without us even realizing it. It plays a considerable role in the lives we live, our traditions and cultures. You see, we are duplicating all the time, to some degree. Children duplicate what they see their parents doing and hear them saying. Young men often duplicate their father by following in his footsteps, taking up the same line of work or profession.

If you noticed how expert your friend was at sailing or skiing etc. then you would watch and do things the same way. Then when next time you went sailing or skiing you would show a little more expertise. Too easy, isn't it? Imagine you were going to have a new home designed to your very own specification, what would you do? I am sure you would look at everything that was the latest in building fashion. You would look at the latest books, magazines, and builders' brochures, and visit new estates and then take the very best from each, and modify to suit your own requirements. Finally you would bring them all together to realize your own new dream home.

That is how the world progresses, it is what stimulates designers, provides fuel for imagination and progress in all areas of industry and commerce.

It is a similar process with little girls growing up. They watch their mothers cook, sew, knit and make dresses and, without even knowing it, they are duplicating. Watch even the smallest little girl and observe how even, at a tender age, her gestures and mannerism's and womanly ways are remarkably like her mum's.

Little boys are no exception. They love to get dirty, dig holes, and tinker with the car's engine like Dad. They look forward to growing hair on their chin like him and developing muscles in their arms, thereby drawing pride from their manly strength.

Don't Duplicate the Negative

Most people act in very much the same way and it probably accounts for the fact that most of the nation's population are either dead or still working at the age of 65. Very, very few will have become successful enough to have retired as the result of generating their own wealth. Most often it is not their fault, it is simply that they followed on from the person who went before them. They led their lives along the same pattern, they duplicated their way of life, and when it turned out to be a failure way of life, that involved them working throughout their life until they dropped. That is exactly what was duplicated.

What often happens when people start out in life is that they look around for help. They see what a hard life their folks had and they want to change the pattern – they want more. That's great. They look around for advice. Their mind is hungry for information. Most often they listen eagerly to whoever will talk to them on the subject. This of course is fine, provided that their mentor is a successful person, which very often he is not. This is the area where the wrong things are often duplicated, where someone has been led up the wrong path.

Fair enough, what happened was unintentional, the wrong advice was given but with the best possible intention (and perhaps love). So – if the person giving it is not a success, how can you know the information is good?

Well, if it were sound advice the person imparting the information would be a success. So before absorbing information that is freely given check that the source of it has 'fruit on its tree'. If your adviser has little to recommend him or is 'broke' then to listen to his advice would be a case of the blind leading the blind. Hard words, but that is how it is and to listen to those people is not too smart because if their information was good then they would be successful.

If you wanted to be a brain surgeon, would you ask a carpenter how to gain access to someone's brain? I don't think you would, but if you did, it would not be very smart. In fact that example is ridiculous but no more ridiculous than asking someone who is 'broke' how to earn your fortune.

The way to learn success is from someone who is already a success. That is such an important statement, you should underline it, read it again and remember it.

LEARN SUCCESS FORM THOSE WHO ARE ALREADY A SUCCESS.

Business is Simple

Successful business is basically very simple if you remember duplication. If you buy an item for £3 and sell it for £4 you have made a healthy profit and on course for a successful business. You have earned £1 profit. If you want to earn £100 then you duplicate the process one hundred times. Alternatively, you can buy an item for £300 and sell it for £400; you have still made one hundred pounds but this time by only making one sale. That, in a nutshell, is how a successful business works.

Let us use the analogy of a major supermarket operation again. To begin with the company opens a single store and operates that until all the bugs and problems have been ironed out and it becomes profitable. Then once that company has one success, it is a simple matter to duplicate that success as many times as required. Each success will be duplicated into another success, and that is the surest and most reliable way to the top.

The procedure will naturally vary a little from profession to profession and trade to trade. Manufacturing trades need a slightly different approach because of high setting-up costs. Doctors, lawyers and other professional people would again vary in their methods, but the concept is the same.

Business can be made as complex and technical as you like. A whole vocabulary of new and frightening words can be brought into the process. 'Profit and loss accounts', 'ledgers', 'files' and 'tax' are all words that may be fired at you, and some may even go above your head. Do not be daunted, business is simple, so do not let that new language deter you.

I have already explained how simple it is and if it involves £3 or £3 million the process is the same. Buy for one price and sell with a profit. It really is that simple.

Do I hear you say, "Yes, but what can I sell?" Well of course that is the sixty-four thousand dollar question, but in my research and experience one little snippit of wisdom repeatedly rises to the top. "Find something that people want and supply it. Find or make a demand then fill it." I agree it is all pretty obvious stuff but when I look about me at some of the schemes people get involved with, I still wonder, is it so obvious?

If you wanted to develop a business of your own with a view to becoming rich and successful, would you select an item such as a 'windscreen wiper for spectacle wearers', or some such new and outlandish product to manufacture? (Remember, you will need to be selling your product for 12 months in every year.) No, I wouldn't be in too much of a hurry to sink money into that.

What I would look for if I were in your shoes would be something that is used by as many people as possible, as often as possible. That would give you the biggest potential market. Then once you knew the market then you could use your creative talents to 'wiggle' your way in to claim a piece for yourself. For myself I would sooner be involved in soap or potatoes than the 'windscreen wiper' idea, since every person in this country washes and most eat potatoes every day.

Momentum

Just a word about momentum. When you think about it, just as 'duplication' was obvious, so also is momentum. It is one of those basic points that are so fundamental that they are often overlooked altogether. But I think it is a very interesting and important subject.

As an example, in my own business life I recall a period when I had completed one career and was about to embark on another. During that time I lost momentum. The changes terminated many old habits and routines, lots of people I was used to seeing every day were suddenly not there any more. My brain, used to dealing with a fairly large company, suddenly had time on its hands. Just as a car would slowly come to a halt if the engine was turned off, I too slowly coasted to a complete stop.

Watch the strong men on TV trying to pull a great truck weighing tons. To begin with they struggle and grunt, leaning their, seemingly small, weight against that of the great truck. To begin with the truck remains firmly stationary but after a few minutes of heaving and straining and huffing and puffing, the impossible begins to happen.

The truck begins to move, very slowly at first. Then by dogged determination and persistence plus every ounce of strength the crazy performer can muster, the wheels begin to move a fraction. Then once the truck has momentum, once our friend has overcome the inertia problem, it begins to move, however slowly, and the effort to keep it moving grows less and as the truck gains more and more momentum, so the problem of moving the bulk becomes easier and easier.

Keep it Moving

Careers, business and your life generally can be like that, – the momentum becomes lost. You may see it as ‘falling flat’ or maybe you have your own term for it. Simply it means that things have lost momentum and, as I have already said, things just cannot remain static. If steps are not taken to stimulate momentum again, then the reverse will happen, you will begin to slide backwards.

But again if you become aware of that problem soon enough, it is a simple matter to relight the fire of enthusiasm or to overcome that situation because as I’ve already explained, it is easier to keep things on the move and progressing than it is to let them grind to a halt and have to start again from scratch.

Business in particular is like that. Those already with business experience will readily know that to start a new business from nothing can be a formidable task. It can take some time before the inertia is overcome and it begins to move along easily. But once under way, once it is moving, things become easier and the more momentum you can achieve the greater your control and the easier it will be for you to progress. In fact, once enough momentum has been gained the project will continue, for short periods, on its own.

So an encouraging word to those setting out in business and finding the going hard: Keep going and never, never give up. Everyone has to overcome this, the law of inertia, before things begin to happen for them. We all have to motivate and get ourselves going, overcome our own personal inertia and attain momentum before we can savour the sweetness of success, and the harder that overcoming process the more enjoyable will be the success. I promise.

One Pair of Hands

One small yet very valuable point worth keeping in mind is, simply, that we only have one pair of hands. If your goal is to become the owner of a large, successful company remember – YOU only have one pair of hands. You could be the best craftsman in the world or the best ladies' hairdresser, but your income is restricted to what YOUR own two hands can produce. So, if your business is dependent upon that, then its output will be severely restricted.

I can recall the situation in the early days when as a boatbuilder my business depended totally upon what my hands could produce. This fact was never more obvious than at holidays or break times, when, the moment I set down my tools, my income stopped. People in business like that just do not get paid for doing nothing. There is no free lunch.

That illustrates the point I've just made about having but 'one pair of hands'. Other examples could include the doctor, dentist, artist, anyone whose skills cannot be easily duplicated. Imagine the frustration of the dentist who wants to expand his practice. He is restricted to how many patients he can personally attend to. On the other hand, if we take the owner of a supermarket who wishes to expand, it is for him simply a matter of employing extra staff, increasing the size of the building and advertising, etc. The supermarket boss is also far less limited because many of the jobs he requires to be done he can delegate to others who in turn can learn by duplication.

Remember that if you want to enjoy the privileges and freedom that a business of your own can offer, you must be able to delegate much of the work, and make the business work for you. As the brain behind the business your time is best utilized in creative areas; the more run-of-the-mill, everyday jobs can be done by someone else.

In the next chapter I will be looking at another topic that is often neglected, yet one that affects every person in the world. Life would be so much more pleasant and rewarding if some of the valuable secrets of FEAR, WORRY AND STRESS were understood.

Some points from this chapter:

- You can if you try.
- Don't counsel with fools.
- Duplicating a profession.
- Duplicating the new.
- Beware of duplicating the negative.
- Business is simple.
- Momentum.
- One pair of hands.

Chapter 6

Fear, Worry or Stress

When fear, worry or stress rear their ugly heads take action against them quickly. Do something about them at once. George didn't slay the dragon by calling it names from behind a tree, he took out his sword and cut its head off. That was that, end of problem and look how famous George became!

Everyone is vulnerable to stress. You may be a corporate director or a labourer, but you can still become a victim of stress. It can be due to overwork or being out of work; stress can even come from boredom.

If you think you are in high stress job or profession, then you are. On the other hand if you really enjoy what you do and can't wait to go to work, then the stress level will be minimal.

Some thrive in a stressful situation, many just do not work at their best until they have reached one. They come to life and do their best work under pressure. Others just cannot function at all under those conditions. Strangely many of those who suffer most from stress are those who have not become successful. The 'almost-made-its.'

So what causes stress? Simply anything is the short answer to that. Anything that is difficult for you to understand or anything you dislike intensely can be the cause. The overdraft at the bank, for instance, the weeds growing three feet tall in the front garden, or simply being caught in a traffic jam on the way to work – they can all be potential causes of stress and worry. Statistics show that more than 50% of illnesses have a stress related factor, and can be the cause of many health problems.

The Stressed Body

When we are worried or under stress the heart pumps faster, the breathing quickens, adrenalin begins to flow, blood is denied to the brain in favour of the muscles and limbs. The blood pressure increases, nerves become tense, muscles tighten ready for physical action. Brain function becomes less effective since it is working on reduced blood supply. This can have both positive and negative effects.

Stress can cause the heart to palpitate, muscles to tremble and quiver, the digestive system to stop working, causing indigestion, heartburn, etc. and the flow of blood generally to fluctuate and become irregular. Outward signs can be exhibited by crying, blushing, sleepiness, etc. Other effects displayed in temper or rage can be blushing or becoming flushed. In extreme fear the face drains of colour, it is very common to shed tears of happiness or sorrow or even be physically sick at things repulsive.

Positive Fear

Some stress can be turned to advantage, if, for example, you are an athlete, boxer, footballer, etc., because your body has received that extra 'oomph'; has increased its performance through both physical and mental boosts.

But if you are a businessman or woman and you find yourself in a stressful situation, it could be that you lost your temper or just allowed it to rise; then you will be in a very negative or minus situation. Like the boxer who drops his guard, you leave yourself wide open to problems.

The brain is then in no condition to think problems out quickly, even to reason and draw facts and logic together. In this physical stage the body will not cope. If you find yourself in this situation and in competition, your handicap is very severe. The person who keeps his cool will control the situation.

Relax

So how can stress be handled? One way is to visit the doctor for a bottle of pills. That can, in the short term, bring relief, but for real control over stress the key word is relaxation. Firstly understand that the more relaxed and in control of your own functions you are the better your position will be, and the greater your chances of success. It is very important to understand this.

It is also of vital importance to know and understand when you are about to lose your cool – but you must pick up the early warning signals, intercept and stop them before they surface. You should never lose your temper.

How can you control that? Once you feel the heartbeat rate quicken, the hairs on the back of the neck stand on end, the heart thump or whatever happens for you, take control of yourself by relaxing. Yes, you will regain control if you learn to relax in those situations. Even if you are at a meeting, negotiating or whatever, learn how to relax right there in that particular situation.

Try this Exercise

Let your shoulders go, let your weight sink to the seat of your pants, but most important of all, slow down your breathing rate. By doing these simple things effectively, you will allow more blood to circulate to the brain and get that functioning better. Once you have that working perfectly the greatest and most wonderful tool in the world will be working flat out for you.

Breathing

Most of the time we use only a small proportion of our lung capacity. In a stressful situation the breathing rate can be 30 to 40 beats per minute. Very shallow, short sharp breaths. At the peak of exertion, say after an exhausting run or when you fly off the handle in an uncontrollable rage, the breathing rate could reach 40 to 50 per minute. This would be 'panting', literally gasping for air. The heart-beat in that situation could also be as high as 160–170 beats per minute. Very stressful.

Take the example of driving your car to work in the traffic. Traditionally the general mood is one of impatience and aggravation. Maybe someone cuts-in on you or passes on the inside or whatever. Your temper begins to rise and with it your breathing rate. At this stage, if you had control over your breathing, you would be able to slow down, remain calm and even return that rude sign with a pleasant smile. Impossible, you say? Not at all. Try this simple exercise but learn and practise whilst you are cool, calm and collected. Once you have mastered it, then it will be easy to perform in the high stress situation.

The object is to breathe through the nose long and slow, using all of the lung capacity. It is important to breathe in through the nose. Believe it or not the nose is a very complex piece of equipment, just one of its twenty or so functions is to filter and sort out the air before allowing it in to the lungs. Breathing in through the mouth allows raw untreated air to be gulped down unchallenged.

Exercise

To begin with, breathe in slowly to the count of three, seeing your tummy as an air tank and filling it from the bottom. Take in as much beautiful fresh air as you can, hold it for the count of two, then slowly breathe out. As you do this, relax the base of the neck and shoulders. Feel them relaxing, sagging, sinking. Feel all your skin sagging and relaxing. Even your mouth may wnt to drop open a little. Repeat and practise. Very soon a breathing rate of 7 to 10 breaths per minute should be easily achieved.

To begin with, slow deep breathing may cause, after a short while, the feeling of breathlessness. This will be overcome as the effectiveness of the relaxation is experienced. A little perseverance is all that is required to become accomplished and gain great benefit from this very important process that is taken so much for granted.

An additional benefit will be gained by those who have difficulty relaxing or getting to sleep at night. Just a few moments of this beautifully relaxing exercise will soon have you off deep in the 'land of nod'.

This is a valuable process in combating stress and tension in almost any situation. It can be conveniently put into practice anywhere and any time and carried out without the knowledge of anyone around. Relaxing in this way, in situ, you will find that it can produce an urgency to 'yawn'. Again, a very pleasant and healthy thing to do, though in public or when holding a conversation, it can be construed as boredom or rudeness. So learn to yawn with your mouth closed. True, for a second or two your face will contort and give the appearance that a pebble has lodged in your throat, but it is better than the chasm that appears when you yawn with your mouth open.

Find Your Calm

I am often asked "What should I see when I relax?" So let me explain. Let us assume that you are just beginning your relaxation session. You are sitting or laying comfortably and beginning the unwinding process. Sit quietly and try to induce that lovely feeling of calm and peace. Help your breathing to slow down. As it does so the feeling of calm will expand to encompass the whole you, almost as though it were a protecting umbrella shielding off the bombarding stresses.

As peace comes, gently clear you mind. By the mere fact of trying you will find the best method for you. Try clearing your mind and transport yourself into a lovely warm glow. Enjoy it – just relax and let go – just sag and flop! As thoughts begin to enter your mind, gently swish them away and come back to your warm glow. And once you have experienced the peace and warmth that relaxation brings you will look forward to your sessions.

Having mastered relaxation you will have worry and stress on the run. You will have taken a big step towards having command over your own destiny. But there is one more feature that is often a hide-out for 'nasties' and can cause many more problems than people are often aware of.

Ego

Many are unaware that one of the causes of their problems and worries can be their own Ego, for there are many people who shrink from undertaking what they consider are demeaning tasks when in fact it is their own pride that may be getting in the way of their personal success. For instance, if there was suddenly a fortune to be earned in emptying dustbins there are many people who would be too proud to do that no matter what the reward. To quote the wise words of Solomon, 'Better to get your hands dirty and eat than keep them clean and starve.'

Without delving into the mysteries of Freud and his theories I will just touch on the subject of EGO.

To begin with, what is it and what has it got to do with the winning concept and becoming successful?

The word ego means self-thinking, self-centred, selfish, egotistic, self-opinionated. It is the ego that seeks to satisfy and protect the person. It's that, 'look after yourself' element in our nature.

The ego is one of those psychological conditions that we don't hear too much about in motivational books for the writer's fear of the trap of contradiction. Because it can be just that, a contradiction. In one breath it is said, 'A man is nothing if he has no pride', in the next it is said, 'That man's too proud to get his hands dirty'. Starting a small business of his own is a little demeaning for him. So the ego keeps him working for someone else, where he remains poor but in a position of status.

It is amazing how many people fall into this category and for them their ego is the problem. They often know deep down that what they must do is to start out in business for themselves. They could do for themselves exactly what they do now for their boss, with the difference that the profits would be theirs. But the problem is that it would mean starting at the beginning again, maybe even having to struggle a little. Then of course there is that other old ogre, 'fear of failure'. 'What would my boss say if I tried it and failed? I couldn't bear to go crawling for my job back!' That negative situation will ring true to some. But if you want to succeed DO IT NOW. If you think you will go crawling for your job back, then you will!

Don't worry about your boss, never will he allow a

situation to occur where you will be earning as much as, or more than, he is. So you are like the sheep and the shepherd I talked about earlier. Do something now, action, action, action.

Look Out for Your Pride

Ego is your pride, a little is fine but too much will place you above the level required to start up in business for yourself and will become a problem to you.

If you are too proud to consider starting a modest little business of your own, then you really do have a problem. You may feel that you are worthy of better things, a bigger business perhaps? But you see, it is just not possible to own a big business to begin with, just like that, because a big business is only a small business that has grown.

The giants of industry were not always giants and highly respected men. Would you believe that every single one of them came into the world in exactly the same way as you did? Each and everyone of them was a beautiful, screaming, naked, helpless, babe. That thought alone may bring things into perspective for you.

Do You Set Limits?

Aristotle Onassis didn't always own whole fleets of ships. He knew hardship and hunger. He had to leave his own country to seek the opportunity he wanted. I'm sure he was proud of starting from nothing, I know I am. But there was never any limit to how much effort, tears, and sweat he was prepared to give to achieve what he wanted. He was going to have success, there was never any doubt about it, and he would do ANYTHING to get it. He would do whatever it took, however long it took, pay whatever price it took, to get where he wanted to go. If someone stole all his money or he lost every penny in a deal, it wouldn't matter. He'd start again tomorrow.

When you look at people like that who risk everything – their home, their lives, all they own – just to move them a little closer to the goal, you get some idea how desperately they craved success. They would humble themselves if need be, do anything in fact just to get a foot on that ladder of success or to climb it just one rung. Does that make your efforts seem a little puny?

I've heard people say, "I'd love to have my own business, if only I had the time! It takes me all my time just to earn enough to live." Baloney. What they are saying is, "I can't be bothered. Life is too easy as it is!" They are rating television viewing time as high as success building time. They just cannot see that once you have a successful business that alone will buy you all the other things you require.

Fire-up to Success

When I have a project in my mind it is like a million volts harnessed but trying to get out. I even resent time being wasted eating, sleeping, even going to the loo. At that stage I would do anything to forward the project and I mean anything, because there really is not room for pride and excess ego. The desire to succeed is so great, I become so fired-up to succeed, so preoccupied and single-minded that winning is assured. It is guaranteed because it is impossible to let-up or stop until success is in the bag. Can you feel that excitement – right now? Do you feel like putting this book down and getting on with your particular project? If you do, then I am achieving what I set out to do by writing this book. So if you feel like that, then do it, put the book down and DO IT NOW. Mark the page and come back to it later.

When you get success-charged to that level there ceases

to be such a thing as work. It becomes your whole life. Work and pleasure become one and the same thing. Life becomes so exciting that you look forward to each new day. There is no difference in work and pleasure – for me they are one and the same. Business is the most exciting thing I know. Your self-image and confidence grow by leaps and bounds. You become aware of qualities you are displaying that you never even thought you possessed. You have your first taste of that true winning concept.

Sort the Men from the Boys

Winning becomes the only way out. 'Succeed or die in the attempt' becomes your motto and if success requires shovelling 'unmentionables' into heaps, so be it. Ego – you better get a peg for your nose!

That very process sorts the men from the boys, the talkers from the doers. It is the very process of making winning men and women. An excited winner would never be too proud to pick up a shovel to do that because he knows, once he gets the measure of the job, he will be employing others to do the shovelling for him. But he needed to do it to become familiar with, and to understand, what was involved.

Without you starting in the race there can be no victory when you pass the winning post! That beautiful garden is only beautiful because someone bent over and pulled out all the weeds. That beautiful cabinet in your lounge is only there because someone had the vision to plant a tree.

The overcoming of your problems makes the moment of victory unbelievably sweet. Imagine how Henry Ford would feel to see the business that he created stretching across the world, an empire that helped revolutionize the world, as did the ideas of Edison, Marconi, Baird and countless others. It really doesn't matter how many failures you may have had or will have along the way, you will be remembered only for your success.

Come Alive

Consider this small list of some of the world's greatest businessmen and women: Henry Ford, J. Paul Getty, Aristotle Onassis, Andrew Carnegie, people who have changed the world. They have become legends. But do you know, you still have the advantage over every single one of them because they are all dead, and you are alive. The most precious gift in the world is – Life itself. No matter how many countless millions those tycoons may have had, or how powerful they may have become as a result, you still have that greatest of all advantages. You're alive today, and you have everything it takes to be whatever you want to be. Choose to be in command of your own destiny. Decide that you will call the tune, not dance like the monkey.

The Eyes can't Lie

Much can be learned from observing the eyes. Already, without knowing it, you know a great deal about the information reflected in the eyes. You know by instinct when someone is angry or just cross or happy or sad. Next time you want to know if someone is motivated or excited about something, look closely at their eyes, because that is the dominating feature.

It is a fact that the pupils of the eyes dilate or get bigger when we become excited or something arouses us. So the eyes are a give-away to the person's emotional state, they reflect naturally the reaction of one's state of mind, and that's very difficult to fake.

Learn from Your Pupils

As a matter of interest, it is reckoned that we humans are more attracted to other humans with large pupils. Have you ever wondered why the most romantic meetings are often set in dimmed light? Why night clubs and other romantic settings are invariably dimly lit? Well, in poor light the pupils of the eyes dilate, they grow larger, making a person much more attractive, particularly to the opposite sex.

Large, dilated pupils, reveal arousal and interest, which again tend to make a person look more attractive. It causes more reaction and interaction between two people and is a big factor in so-called hypnotic personality.

The more we look and gaze at each other the more intense the feeling between two people becomes. That explains why lovers gaze into each other's eyes a great deal. The more a person gazes at you the more they tend to like you, although it must be said that anger and uneasiness can be expressed in the same way. Nevertheless the eyes reveal very clearly which end of the spectrum they are operating at.

So much information can be transmitted by the eyes that a little study of them can be well worth your while because it can give a very clear insight into the other person's innermost feelings.

Switch Stress to Positive

If you try, it is easy to turn stress into a positive – another instance in which the negative can be turned around and used to advantage.

I remember when I first began writing. I made no secret of my scribblings or of my goals in that direction. Everyone knew what I was aiming for and patiently endured me (well most did!). There were those who, for some reason, thought it was funny. To them I was the subject of much 'mickey-taking', 'dream-stealing', call it what you will.

They would call me Will Shakespeare, or Ian Fleming, who were the only writers they had ever heard of. A little friendly gibing is fun, and well within my stress threshold, but continued to the degree of becoming personally insulting does jade even the strongest will.

The more they laughed the more determined I became to 'show 'em'. True I had stand-up battles with them and many verbal punch-ups. But they never stopped, and the flow of gibes just kept on coming. Yet the more they did the more certain I was that success as a writer would be mine. From that period of my life in the boatyards my efforts to get published doubled.

Those boatbuilders will never know how grateful I am now for all that, because they gave me the fire and desperation needed to succeed. There was no question about it, I just HAD to succeed or I would never again be able to hold my head up. I can remember every single one of the scoffers. I don't see them too often now because they still work in the boatyard!

Depression

No one is immune to depression, it is something that creeps up on us all at some time. But again, you must be in control, know what to do. When depression strikes it must be moved on again as quickly as possible and the quickest antidote is ACTION. Do something.

When everything seems to be going wrong (and every once in a while it does), things just seem to fall apart, it never rains but it pours, as they say. You become the victim of an avalanche of problems, usually negative ones. Often these are silly little niggly things that just should not bother you at all.

The sure-fire answer is to get on and DO something, get on the move. Don't sit about thinking about how flat you feel and wondering what is going to be the next thing to go wrong. Involve yourself in something. Become absorbed in a project, anything, even digging the garden, just something.

This sudden extra burst of positive energy will have the effect of blowing the cobwebs and negatives away. Add to this an excited feeling, just feel excited, refuse to be blown flat. You are a winner. You have control. Don't give the negative dust time to settle, get up-and-at-'em.

In the next chapter I will be dealing with attitude and faith, two items that are vital to the seeker of success.

Points from this chapter:

- Learn to relax.
- Breathing exercise.
- Sort the men from the boys.
- Fire-up to success.
- Look out for your pride.
- Find your calm.
- The eyes have a message.

Chapter 7

Attitude

"When he was good he was very very good, but when he was bad he was horrid!" That is a quotation that my mother would relate with regularity. I'm not sure if this was a direct reflection on my boyish attitude or not but it is true that most people are like that. When things are going well everything falls into place, they just seem to flow right, as though by magic. And when they go wrong – everything seems to fall about your ears.

I recall just a short while ago talking to some dear friends of mine about 'getting into action and making things happen'. Our conversation is always open and friendly and we enjoy the respect of each other without the formalities. We were talking about getting publicity and making opportunities for a project.

"Some people just seem to fall on their feet," said Sam, doubting his own abilities to get things on the move.

"The answer is to get out and DO something. Get into action," I said.

"What sort of action?" Sam mused.

"Any action is better than no action," I rounded on him. "Just DO something, take the initiative. You can never go anywhere without doing something, making a move."

"If you want somewhere to go, you can return my library books." Sam's wife overhearing what we were talking about capitalized on the situation.

"Sure, that's fine, anything is better than doing nothing or watching the 'idiot' box."

Fate at Work?

So we headed for the library and after parking the car we noticed a huddle of people at the entrance. Moving closer we noticed the interest was created by a TV crew filming. To our amazement we found the great 'eye' of the camera on us and we were interviewed and asked our opinions on some local issues. On completion of the interview I got into conversation with the producer, who was asking all the questions. I introduced Sam as the manager of a Publishing Company, whereupon his ears pricked up, and as a result Sam got some valuable TV coverage and an invitation to take part in another programme.

Sam could not believe his luck. He marvelled all the way home at his sudden change of fortune.

"But that is just the point, Sam," I said. "You made that luck, you made something happen with action. Simply by being positive, by going out and doing something, getting into action, things began to happen."

It is my opinion that by doing that you are giving the brain and your 'inner-self' the opportunity it needs to go to work. If the brain is kept programmed with what is required it will not stop searching and working on it until it has success. But it can achieve nothing if everything is static and immobile. With a positive attitude you can keep things on the move and progressing.

Things like that often happen for me. Time after time I marvel at the way fortune takes a hand in the more positive events of my life. Is it coincidence? Maybe, but I like to think that it is something more than that. I have heard people say, "It's amazing how he just keeps falling on his feet." Sometimes it irritates me because I have to explain how it works and how THEY can do it, how anyone can do it. Yet still they do nothing, save continue to moan. Oh well, 'there's none so queer as folk'.

Make Your Own Luck

There is no doubt in my mind at all that you can control the situation to a great degree. You can make your own luck, simply by having a positive mental attitude and manipulating yourself into situations conducive to those things you require. Just get amongst it, and from the beginning you are in with a chance, maybe just a slim chance, but more of a chance than you would have if you sit at home on your 'butt'.

Get to know what you want and KNOW you are going to get it. Be positive about it. You can if you think you can. Remember? So stop 'pussy-footing' about and go for it. If you need information or help in the business or financial fields then frequent establishments used by the type of person who can help you and offer good advice. Maybe a yacht club or a country club. On the other hand, if you are after information on truck drivers, look for a transport café. That is just common sense, isn't it? Make things happen, you're in charge.

What is the Right Attitude?

With the right attitude it is possible to achieve some amazing things. But what IS the right attitude? Well, everything about you contributes in some way. If you exude a pleasant personality and show an interest in other people, often they will respond by going out of their way to help YOU. The most important person in everyone's live is themselves. So, genuinely show interest in the other person, by being a good listener, then there's a good chance of them responding warmly and positively towards you. You may have been having a really tough time with your business but when someone asks, "How are you doing?" answer with enthusiasm, "I'm feeling great, how about you?" That is having a positive attitude, try it and persevere because it really does work. Keep at it until it becomes a habit and is done quite naturally.

If I employ someone who 'only just' does what he or she is paid to do, no more no less, then I watch them closely because they are usually the 'clock watchers' and often completely disinterested in the job. They have a very poor attitude. This type of person will often take advantage, given the opportunity. On the other hand, the person who 'goes the extra mile', who makes the effort to please, to do a good job, has a positive attitude. That kind of person is alert, always on the move, interested in what he is doing. He has 'zap' and enthusiasm, both qualities that generate good relations and a pleasant working environment.

How to Keep the Attitude Right

At this stage people often say, "Oh that's easy to say, but how do you always keep in a good mood?" Well, the positive atittude works best when you manifest it without even thinking. When it's a natural habit. When you don't even have to think about replying to a question in a positive way. When you learn to listen with interest to the other person's story. Simply by listening and showing an interest you will be 'marked up' in most people's esteem.

For the next day or two just be aware of that point and take note. Many, many times I have seen it happen, that just because someone has been a willing listener and showed an interest in the other person, the response has been, "Gee, what a great guy!" And all because someone listened. The big plus is that the next time you meet that person you can be sure they'll be on your side.

Start the Day Right

So often when things start off on the wrong foot they continue like that for the rest of the day or week. So learn to take control. Start the moment you open your eyes in the morning, when the slate is clean; and fill it only with good positive information. Think really good enthusiastic things, right from the start. "Hey, I really feel good today, boy am I going to make things happen!" Leap out of bed and be cheerful and enthusiastic, refuse to be miserable. Give the cat a cuddle instead of a kick. Your wife will be amazed and delighted when you give her a kiss instead of moaning that your coffee is cold and your shirt is not pressed.

You'll be amazed at the knock-on effect it has. Your wife will say, "Here, let me make you a fresh cup of coffee, darling," instead of "Tough, you let it get cold . . ." Even the cat will stay about instead of making a bolt for the door. When you are stuck in traffic and everyone about you is fuming and fretting, hating just about everything in sight, that genuine smile has an unbelievable effect. When that driver behind leans on his horn and yells all those compliments at you, you will be amazed at the effect of a broad 'I love you smile' and a cheery "Good morning!"

The effects are amazing and so much fun. Try it, try changing everything around to the positive. Refuse to let other people's negatives get to you, do THEM a favour and change their negatives around to positives. When you hear that gloomy voice say, "Uuugh, it's Monday again," come back with, "Yeah, aint it great! We got a whole new week untouched."

Most of the negatives we come up against are simply

silly habits. For some reason Monday mornings just have to be lousy, and sitting in the traffic has to be a time of hate. I wonder why?

In many respects the brain is like a tape-recorder. On the tape is stored all the information you wished to keep and refer to. The instruction on how you will conduct yourself and your thinking during the day, including your habits both good and bad, will probably be old and outdated. It may have been put there long ago in some very negative period or even arrive there in error, but the fact is, it's there. So, as anyone with a tape-recorder knows, if you want to change the message on the tape, all that is required is to feed in the new information and automatically the old, negatives, are removed. So from that point on every time the recorder is turned on the new positive information begins to flow out. The last chapter will give more detailed information on that.

Positives In, Negatives Out

Think of your brain like that and start to change those negatives around. Already you have begun by reading this book and by repeated 'doses' of the positive medicine you can overcome and replace the store of negatives you already have in your brain. Like a computer, feed your brain rubbish and negative information and that is exactly what you will get back out. You get what you give, rubbish in, rubbish out.

Start feeding your brain stimulating positive thoughts, become enthusiastic and vital. Improve the quality of your thinking. Read and listen to motivational material on a regular basis and you will be feeding your brain the food for success. Simply adopting a positive attitude will, without question, change your whole life. You will find that other people with the same attitude will be attracted to you. People of the old negative gang will not be attracted to you, they will go elsewhere and search out the negatives. Like attracts like.

And guess what: people with a positive attitude are successful people and success breeds success. Mix with winners and you'll be a winner. So, simply be changing to a positive mental attitude you will travel along the road to success and open up opportunities you never before thought possible. After all, what choice do you have? on the one hand is gloom and despondency with everyone and everything negative and downbeat, on the other your world can be full of laughter and good cheer with life a fun thing and very upbeat.

Form the positive habit. Beginning NOW, exercise control over the way you think. Work hard at developing that positive attitude. Habits are formed by repetition, by repeating and correcting over and over again. Just as a single strand of cotton has very little strength but by looping it round and round, as when sewing on a button, it becomes incredibly strong. Start to form new positive habits now.

Edification

Another area to look at for positive change is in people. All too often when one person talks about another it is in the negative. But why? I think it is just a silly habit and not a very adult practice at all. It has a de-edifying, demeaning, putting-down effect. So what happens when someone discovers that you have been putting them down? They begin to slang you and put you down in return. And without even knowing it you are both looking for the negative in each other to use as ammunition. You are verbally pummelling each other into submission. How silly and destructive that is!

Reverse the situation and watch the results. Instead of 'knocking' everyone let's edify them, and look for the good in them. Now what effect will that have? Well, when someone discovers that you have been talking about them again but this time it has been all good there will be a different response entirely. Your compliments will have fallen on fertile soil and in all probability have produced a crop of golden compliments in return. In short, you have been spreading the positive instead of the negative. If everyone would do that just once every day, wow! what a difference it would make!

Are you happy?

In this section I want to bring together some of the things that make a winning concept. I make no apology if I duplicate some of the items already covered. Repetition is good. In the end everyone is seeking the same objective, happiness. Just what happiness means for you is a personal point that only you can decide upon. I think it was Abraham Lincoln who said; "People are as happy as they make up their minds to be."

Have you made up your mind how happy you want to be? Do you know exactly what YOU want out of life, in detail? Your journey to that success cannot begin until you know exactly where it is you want to go, and what you want to achieve. Everything in life is like that, you must know what you want before you can attain it. (Chapter One.)

Winners

When the car goes wrong every care and remedial exercise is carried out until it is back in full running order, the mechanic will help you with that. When we are sick all the systems are checked to find exactly what the problem is and then what is needed to restore ourselves to health.

The doctor will help with that. But how many spend their lives in misery and failure, being without the success they really need? Yet because they do not have success they do nothing about it, they do not have access to a 'Success doctor' or even understand why, or what the problem is, nothing happens – nothing is done.

At this stage many consider that life has failed them, that they have been dealt a losing hand. Some blame failure on fate, even worse, on God. They become engulfed in the downward spiral, ever decreasing – negatives pile upon negatives. Goals and dreams become the subjects of ridicule and lack any credibility.

Just a while ago I was delighted to have the opportunity to help a couple of great guys to start up in a business of their own. They were doing great, the business was slowly gaining momentum, little by little things were beginning to happen for them. So determined were they to lift their lives above their lowly position as dustmen, they worked hard and long. They had wonderful goals, they bubbled with excitement and imagination; truly they were a joy to be with. Everything was in order and moving forward nicely, success was just a while away.

Then, as occasionally happens in life, they went through a bumpy patch. They had one or two negative situations to overcome, their ego took a knock. They took all the negatives as being personally aimed at them, and rather than parrying the blows and warding off the negative, it was permitted to lay them low and they succumbed to the 'knocks'.

Overnight their confidence was lost, their self-image took a nose dive and their enthusiasm plummeted. I think I was more shattered than they were; they had completely given up, just like that.

"But why?" I asked in disbelief.

"I knew, deep down, that it wouldn't last. We were just kidding ourselves. We're just dustbin men and that's the end of it. People won't ever us forget it." I found it difficult to believe my ears, such a turn-around was unbelievable.

"Whoever it was that upset you is trying to steal your future. Because they were not doing what you were doing, they were jealous," I said. "Your attitude at the start was what set you on your course as dustmen. But you had it whacked, you were winning, you had lifted yourselves out of that losing situation. You can't give up just like that!"

"Naaa, they'll never let us forget it . . ." It was too late, they had blown out their own candle. They had given up at the first fence, with the first objection, the first sign of a struggle. They had lost faith and nothing I could say would change their minds.

That is a true story, and sadly it is all too common. I relate it here as a warning of what can happen when the negative takes over, when you lose out to weakness. So that as you begin to carve out your success YOU will not turn and run when YOU have a cold blast of the negatives. Instead, you will face the test whatever it is. Square those shoulders and remember that you are a WINNER and there is nothing anyone can throw at a winner that he can't overcome one way or another. Be determined to do whatever it takes and however long it takes. The rewards are worth it.

Act on Faith

Many times in my business-life I have come up against situations that looked impossible, and quite truthfully they are frightening; they place you under pressure. I can't say I have enjoyed those experiences at the time, but once they have been overcome it has been very satisfying to look back and say, "Pheeew! I did it." The very process helps you to stretch and grow. It is the quickest and surest way to build self-image and confidence.

But don't imagine that all life's problem must be faced alone. True, so many people do – they worry and struggle, wondering what to do, when very often all they need to do is ask! I have many friends in business and I can say with honesty that if I need to know something, and I often do, I have no hesitation in asking. Most often they are only too delighted to be able to help. Try it, you'll be glad you did.

But just one word of caution, be sure that whomever you ask for help has the answer. Don't counsel with fools; if your desire is for money don't ask the advice of a person who is broke. If his advice were any good, why is HE not rich? Check what apples he has on his tree before trusting his word. On the other hand, when you seek the advice of a rich and successful man, then listen and DO as he says, because he knows what he is talking about.

Everyone needs that help, that leg-up, but be sure that your counsellor is qualified to give it. The world is full of talented talkers who love telling everyone else what to do, but rarely have they made the grade themselves.

What's it All About?

It's a normal human reaction to want the best out of life, or what in a word this book terms success. But what is success? Is it an accumulation of great wealth, or the possessing of all the longed for luxuries that have become the tangible evidence of success? No. Success is the person, the man or woman. Material effects is the PROOF of his or her success, not the success itself. Very often the more material luxuries a person accumulates, the greater the indication of his wealth. Possessions could be considered the yardstick or measure of success. But success is not always material.

Success may be an outlet for a great talent that you feel is hidden deep in your store of untapped resources. That unopened vault within, that holds those hidden dreams.

They may even be dreams and desires that you are not even aware of. You may be suppressing talents that you did not even know possessed. You may be hiding a magical singing voice that equals the great Caruso's or the artistic genius of Constable or the musical magic of Beethoven, Bernstein or McCartney, who knows?

I'm sure that in your heart you have felt at sometime that you possess qualities that, allowed to surface, are special. You have felt, or you are feeling right now, that you could be a great success if only . . .

I always felt like that. I always knew that I would find that 'something' I could excel in. I knew I had a talent that could be developed and nurtured until it was strong enough to lift me on to the level to which I considered was my rightful place in society.

Believe me, dear reader, you also HAVE that talent. It may still be locked away in that hidden store, undiscovered, untapped, but it is there, no doubt about it. Is it going to be like a beautiful flower that grows, fades and dies in the wilderness, without it ever being seen by an admiring eye, without its ever having touched another person's life or even made them aware of its existence? Like a man locked in prison, whose life, like the flower wilting, is wasting and passing without notice? Or without even exposing its existance. Are you like that? Do you have a secret yen to do or be something special? You will never know unless you try.

Those feelings and ambitions, even if you don't know what they are, are the seeds of the future. You will never know what beauty those seeds may produce if you never plant them and nurture them.

People fall into two groups:

A. Those who are aware of the talents and hidden skill and desires that lay locked away deep within but have not been able to release them or help them to flower and produce the fruits of their desires.

B. Those who, for one reason or another, are not aware of the eagle of freedom and achievement that is roosting deep within. They are not aware of their own capabilities and possibilities. Only aware that "I must be good at something, if only I knew what!"

For those people who can identify with Group B, the following may be of help. Re-read Chapter Three, in particular THAT GUT FEELING. Instruct your inner self to help you find what it is you are looking for. Sincerely and irrevocably seek this information. Then open your mind and imagination, and just relax and forget about everything. You will be surprised at what may present itself.

Understand, that inspiration received in this way may arrive at any time or place. Often in the most unlikely situations, so be receptive to all suggestions, 'gut feelings' and other unusual thoughts.

Finish the Race

Just a small point but a very important one springs to mind as I near the end of this book. The progress of this very book can be likened to most struggles, be it building a business, a game of football, even the making of a lovely garden.

I can tell you that I have lived for almost a year now with the words of this book, producing a little more each and every day, one step at a time. Up to this time around thirty-six thousand words have made the grade to the finished page. Thousands more have made hasty exits via my wastepaper bin.

Although my enthusiasm never wanes once I set out to produce a new book, there is the time, towards the end, when the creative work of the writer is complete and the more mundane tasks of producing the end product, the book, must be completed. Writing the words and assembling them on paper and eventually into manuscript form is just one part of producing a book.

There also have to be negotiations with printers, whose proof readers perform their unique skills in correcting the manuscript for spelling, grammar and syntax. In addition, the book needs to be registered with the British Library, so that it can be allocated an ISBN number for reference purposes. The all-important cover has to be designed. Brochures, leaflets, press hand-outs, review information and one hundred and one other but very important details must be attended to.

For me this is the drudgery of producing a book and the whole point of this illustration. If I just produced the interesting and creative part, the manuscript, and then lost interest, nothing would ever have happened. The book would never have seen the light of day. All my words would have gathered dust on the shelves of my office. It has to be completed, distributed, advertised and displayed on the bookshop shelf before the job is done.

If you are playing a game of football and your team is well ahead ten minutes before time, you cannot leave the field or stop playing, however sure you are of success. You must keep going until the final whistle, until the job is done, before you succeed.

Business and success are like that too. You may have the most sure-fire deal all stitched up that indicates that nothing can go wrong! But you would be foolish to crow or start to spend the profits of your success until everything was complete and the cheque has been put in the bank and cleared. Only then can you claim success. Like a jig-saw puzzle the pretty picture is not complete until the last piece is in place.

Looking on the other side of the coin, if your life up to this point has not been everything you would have hoped for, then set about changing things now. It's not too late, the final whistle hasn't been blown yet. There is always time to succeed if you would just free yourself from those invisible chains that have manacled you until now. The key that will free you from those chains is simply the will to stand up and say, "By golly I'm worthy of better things than I've got now, and what's more I'll show everyone that I CAN do what it takes. I'll show 'em." Look for that missing piece of jig-saw puzzle.

That desperate act holds the secret. There is a telling story of the Greek philosopher Socrates who held one of his pupils under the water until in desperation the pupil fought and struggled desperately to the surface. "Why did you do that?" asked the pupil. "To show you that, if you want real success, that is how desperately you must want it." And there you have the answer, the secret of success. Want your success desperately. Remember the struggle of that drowning man and search for your success with the same desperation. Then you will win, I promise.

You may now to able to see why those in real poverty often reach the pinnacle of success when others, more privileged but with a softer life-style, miss out. It is because those less privileged needed to be more desperate in their pursuit of success. The classic example is of the many black boxers born in abject poverty in the United States who literally fought their way out of the ghettoes to become wealthy and successful boxers.

Look for your goals and become so desperate to achieve them that you will find that desperation. Be enthusiastic. You can do it, and the feeling of achievement when you have, will make everything seem so worth while. The prize of success will taste so much sweeter, you will have grown and stretched so much, you will feel so satisfied, that you will be able to look into the mirror and say, "Did I really do that? What d'you know, I made it. I AM a success."

In the final chapter I will cover some of the benefits and techniques of achieving relaxation. And how to make it work for you and why it is so important.

Some points from this chapter:

- Fate at work
- Make your own luck
- How to keep your attitude right
- Positives in, negatives out
- Edification
- Are YOU happy?
- Act on faith
- Finish the race

Chapter 8

Relax

Relax and become a Winner

This final section of my winning concepts I want to devote to the all-important subject of relaxation. It is my view that business people need to spend a little time alone in peace and quiet. Time to think for the entrepreneur is essential. It is where those ideas and schemes are conceived, where the miracle of imagination materializes and is set to work. To a thinking person it would seem obvious but for many busy people time to stop and sit down and relax may be brushed aside in favour of action. But, just as the horse must go before the cart, thought and imagination must precede the action. Plan your work, then work your plan. Many are running themselves 'ragged' by not giving themselves time enough to think.

I remember some years ago I was asked to help set up and run a company and I recall having a brush with a fellow director over the fact that I scheduled a half hour of my time every day to be kept free. Time to think and relax. Half an hour, which normally would be whittled away to fifteen minutes, where I could be quiet and relax. Time to sort out what had to be done and in what order of priority. In a word–planning.

What I do, and this works beautifully for me, is to sit quietly and relax. When I feel calm and unwound I take an inward look at the details of problems on hand. If it is the day-to-day running of a business, I look at the details and tasks to be done that were previously buzzing about my brain like peas in a bucket, but now I can look at them in a calm and orderly fashion. Then I can write them down on to a piece of paper in the order in which they must be completed. Then I can rejoin the world, after just about fifteen minutes, with a plan of exactly what is going to be achieved and when. And as an extra bonus, I feel as fresh as a daisy and ready to go.

Armed with my list I can mark those items that demand my personal attention and the rest can be delegated to others for action. This means that I can devote all my attention to the important things I am going to do, without wondering, "Have I forgotten this?" or "Did I remember to order that?"

Focus the Brain

Once I had learned to relax and take charge of my own brain the advantages were manifold. One of the advantages I can pass on was of inestimable value to me. This method is used to crack single problems. In my profession I often came up against technical problems that, at first sight, seemed insurmountable, but I found that when alone and relaxed I could focus ALL my brain's attention on the one single problem, and I often came up with solutions that were sometimes so imaginative and 'clever' that I even amazed myself!

It is like the analogy of the magnifying glass focusing the sun's rays on to a single point – the heat becomes so intense that it can create fire. Similarly all the brain's amazing capacity concentrated on a single problem will very often 'crack it'. I have used this many many times and always to advantage.

The Secret Within

Without question YOUR rise to success will start from the moment you SEE yourself as a success, doing what you want to succeed at. In other words, once you can see clearly what it is you want to achieve, then, and only then, will you begin to move forward and progress towards your goals. I have already covered this to some degree in the first chapter but there are two remaining methods that could prove important to you. They are through the medium of:

1. Relaxation
2. Affirmation

It is common sense to apply what works best for you. It could be one method or a combination of several.

Relax

I hear people say, "Oh if only I could relax – I feel so strung-up." Have YOU felt like that? I'm sure you have, and in that condition you were far from being at your best. In fact, you were probably feeling very 'low'. Well, when you learn to relax properly those tensions and stresses will be easily controlled and overcome.

Being creatures of habit, relaxation becomes easier the more we do it. So if you form a habit of relaxing for a short period each day you will gain great benefit and exercise much more control over your own life. Even more important is the fact that it is very pleasant, and I feel sure, once you have tried, you will look forward to your daily session on your own.

When

Very often our lives are ruled by alarm clocks and schedules but it is possible to relax at any time and as you become more proficient you will be able to relax almost anywhere – at the office, in the train, just about anywhere. But please remember NEVER PRACTISE RELAXATION EXERCISES WHILST DRIVING or whilst operating machinery or in any situation where full alertness is required.

The two best times to relax are in the morning before going to work and last thing at night before going to sleep. People who have a problem 'dropping off' will find it invaluable. In fact the very reason you have difficulty going to sleep is because you say you do – you get what you speak, remember? So the best advice I can offer insomniacs is – forget about it, don't worry, just relax.

There are two very distinct advantages in learning to relax. The first is the obvious benefit to the body whereby you are able to unwind and release those pent-up tensions and anxieties – it's a delight just to be able to completely RELAX. Those who have never really relaxed before will love the experience and soon understand just how tensed and under stress their body and brain have become. I often liken it to a tightly wound spring of a clock that just needs to unwind and release the tension for a while.

The Magic Left and Right

The other advantage may not be so obvious at first but could prove of great help to you in your journey to success. You see, (to keep things non-technical), our brain is in two halves, the left and right hemispheres, and it is the left side that controls the majority of the natural functions of our waking day: moving, walking, eating, speaking, etc.

Now, if we have a problem with any of those things they are sorted out almost without thinking, automatically. For instance if there was an eating problem, eating too much or too little, the left hemisphere of the brain would look after it without any problem. It also deals with the ego.

The right side or hemisphere of the brain is the subconscious and deals with emotions, dreams, imagination, etc. Now if you want to change something that is a right brain function, say with an emotion or the imagination, a situation where both halves of the brain need to be reasonably in tune with each other, then access to the right brain is required. And the easiest way we can get to that is through deep relaxation, when the left side is slowed down, when it is resting, and the right side is preparing itself for its 'night job' of dreaming, etc.

In that lovely relaxed state you can put thoughts or messages into the system via the right side of the brain. Some students even use it to help absorb information for exams and the like.

Once you have mastered this process, information in the form of suggestions may be fed in and some amazing results may come out. I have already explained what a wonderful machine the brain is. Weighing in at about 2.5 pounds there has never been devised a more amazing piece of equipment.

Let us look at some of the ways we can use more of its potential. Remember in Chapter Two I said, "Convince your brain that you ARE a success now?" Well, telling the brain just that – giving it those instructions whilst being beautifully relaxed – will greatly help because you are delivering the message directly to the department of the brain that deals with it, the subconscious. So by relaxing you can introduce the seeds of success right to the very centre of that wonderful machine that can determine your destiny. More about what to feed in, in a moment; first let us tackle the process of relaxation.

A Relaxing Situation

The situation most conducive to relaxation is one of peace and solitude. Somewhere quite free from jangling telephones, children playing or noisy machines working. As you become practised in the art of relaxation so you will be able to cope with these distractions. But to begin with, the more peaceful the setting the better.

Find somewhere you can be alone and free of interruptions, somewhere you know people are not going to come bursting in or knocking at the door, etc. A dimly lit room or one with the curtains drawn is ideal.

Sit or lie on a couch or chair or on the floor. I like to recline in a chair with my head supported. Some like to sit with their back straight, others lie on the floor with a cushion under the head. All that matters is that you are comfortable and able to relax.

Letting Go

Now you are comfortable, begin by deep breathing through the nose as described in Chapter Six. As you do this let your body go, let it sag. Just let go. For a moment see your muscles as the coiled springs of a clock and let them unwind. And as they do, imagine that lurking within the 'leaves' of the spring are all the tensions and anxieties you wish to release. As you relax, and the spring unwinds, so these tensions and anxieties are released. See them as water in the mind's eye and let them flow freely away. See the steady flow of stress and tensions flowing like water from your body and as it does so your body will become more and more relaxed.

The more you do it, the easier it is and the more effective it becomes. Let this lovely feeling spread over the whole of your body, from the top of your head to the tips of your toes. Relax your eyes, let them go, relax the back of the eyes – let your brain relax, the forehead, the muscles of the face, the mouth, shoulders, neck, everything. Just let go completely. Feel each part relax as you progress.

As you become proficient at this part of the exercise so you will find a similar control of what is taking place within the mind. To say "Make your mind a blank!" is a tall order because, as anyone who has tried to do it will know, when you make it a blank all manner of thoughts and pictures creep in. One thing the brain begins to ask is 'What is a blank?' and it starts showing images of blank walls, blank cheques, blank expressions, etc., then of course it is fully occupied again.

The Methods

There are several methods to enable you to relax the brain. Here are some to try:

1. Relax and see in the mind's eye a beautiful orange glow. That's all, just a beautiful orange glow. Then if any thoughts or pictures stray on to it, gently guide them out of the way and return to your orange glow.

Do everything in a gentle, relaxed manner. Don't 'do battle' with your thoughts – simply begin to control them and gently usher them away as you would help an old lady across the street.

2. Another way to calm a troubled mind is to use a 'mantra'. Devotees of this method often have Sanskrit word-sounds which they use as mantras; they all work beautifully. I sometimes use the word 'peace'. Gently see it and repeat it, it is very relaxing. Sometimes I see it as a flower opening gently, and repeating PEACE–PEACE–PEACE. If any thoughts creep in let 'PEACE' gently swish them away.

3. Similar to 2 above but instead of a word or mantra use an image, a simple picture of a beautiful rose, a single

little tree or a yacht becalmed on a still sea. Anything that is peaceful and relaxing.

4. Some like to use the method where a peaceful scene is created in the mind's eye. It can be an idyllic beach with palm trees, a warm breeze, clear tropical water or the solitude of the open countryside with green fields and swaying corn.

Try some of them – you will soon find something that suits you and that you enjoy. Something very private and personal.

Having mastered the process of relaxing to the degree that it can be undertaken successfully almost without thinking about it, then is the time when you can turn its uses to more personal and selective subjects. I have reached the stage myself where I can easily relax. All I need is somewhere quiet, warm and comfortable and soon I can be very deeply relaxed in just a few minutes, using the methods set out above.

This is the stage at which you can begin to be a little more creative. By repeating the affirmations of what you require at this relaxed stage, you will be giving the brain the very instructions you wish it to have.

Warning

I must repeat a warning at this stage. In this very relaxed state the subconcious brain is susceptible to your thought waves. As I have already said, the brain will absorb everything you give it. That of course can be a wonderful asset, but be very particular and selective of the kind of information you feed it. One way to do this is NEVER to use negative words or expressions. Never let your brain receive anything harmful or that has any hint of negatives.

In your affirmations refer only to the positive. For

instance, if you wish to instruct your brain about your thinking try it like this: "From this moment on all my thinking is positive." Rather than: "From this moment on I will try never to use negative thoughts." Although they basically both mean the same thing the first one is the positive and correct approach. In the second sentence both 'try' and 'negative' are NO NO's.

Charisma

In Chapter One we talked about those people who have a presence, an aura, charisma, call it what you will, but how do you get it? How do you achieve those qualities everyone would just love to have? What is it that makes people turn their heads and notice when you pass? If the answer were easy then its elusiveness and its desirability would be diminished. If it could be sold by the box someone would be making a fortune.

Those with charisma are often unaware of it, and it is that unaffectedness that is an integral part of charisma. It is my personal opinion that people with charisma are special people, and I believe that the secret of charisma lies in these three qualities:

1. Self-image (confidence)
2. Positive mental attitude
3. Enthusiasm and excitement

Become strong in these three qualities and you will possess charisma, which is the gift of only an envied few.

All those qualities are described in this book: apply them to yourself with a genuine desire to extend them to all others. Transmit your aura, communicating with your eyes, with love from your very soul to everyone within reach.

Cultivate your brain with all the love you would lavish

on a beautiful garden. Feed it regularly with the best, and plan every detail. In return you will have the use of the most wonderful machine known to man. Once it has been cultivated and brought under control it will require only the minimum of maintenance to keep it beautiful, productive and a joy forever.

Some points from this chapter:

- What is the right attitude?
- Start the day right
- Positive in – negative out
- Edification
- Relax and become a winner
- The secret within
- Charisma

Have you read